THE DIRECT PATH TO HEALING

Also by Dr. Eric Pearl

The Reconnection: Heal Others, Heal Yourself
Solomon Speaks On Reconnecting Your Life (coauthor Frederick Ponzlov)

THE DIRECT PATH TO HEALING

A TRINITY OF ENERGY, LIGHT & INFORMATION

Dr. Eric Pearl and Jillian Fleer

Waterside Productions

ISBN-13: 978-1-958848-40-1 print edition
ISBN-13: 978-1-958848-41-8 e-book edition

Waterside Productions
2055 Oxford Ave
Cardiff, CA 92007
www.waterside.com

DEDICATION

In Loving Memory of Our Parents
Harold and Lois Pearl
and
Jerry and Sheila Kalish
who are smiling, laughing and loving our collaboration.

In loving memory of our beloved "Mama" Pat Atanas.

To all those on this planet living in receivership and recognition of Energy,
Light & Information® who have chosen to help get the world ready instead
of waiting for the world to become ready.

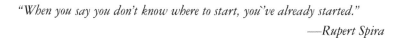

"When you say you don't know where to start, you've already started."
—*Rupert Spira*

ACKNOWLEDGMENTS

To God/Love/Infinite.

SUGGESTED SUPPLEMENTARY READING:

The Reconnection: Heal Others, Heal Yourself
—*Dr. Eric Pearl*

Solomon Speaks On Reconnecting Your Life
—*Dr. Eric Pearl and Frederick Ponzlov*

CONTENTS

Preface ·ix

Introduction ·xi

Before You Read Any Further ... · xv

Chapter 1: The Gift of the Healer · 1

Chapter 2: The Gift of Energy, Light & Information · · · · · · · · · · · · · · · 15

Chapter 3: The Gift of Receiving· 37

Chapter 4: The Gift of Mindful Mindlessness · · · · · · · · · · · · · · · · · · 59

Chapter 5: The Gift of the Coherent Catalyst· · · · · · · · · · · · · · · · · · · 80

Chapter 6: The Gift of Distance · 93

Chapter 7: I AM ... the Healer· 103

PREFACE

*"There will come a time when you believe everything is finished.
That will be the beginning."*

—Louis L'Amour

In 2001, a book called *The Reconnection: Heal Others, Heal Yourself* (Hay House),
written by Dr. Eric Pearl, chronicling the discovery of Reconnective Healing,
was published. It quickly became and remains an international bestseller in
its field in 40 languages. It not only speaks of the exciting and unprecedented
discovery of Reconnective Healing, but of what led up to it, what it is and
some simple basics on how to facilitate it for yourself and for others. It explains
Reconnective Healing as clearly as it was understood at the time. It is honest,
accurate, compelling in its simplicity and makes Reconnective Healing highly
accessible in its basic philosophy and with simple how-to's.

Truth does not change. Our ability to communicate and convey it is,
however, another story.

It is now time to explain the Reconnective Healing Experience—to
explain Healing *itself*—and make it even more accessible in a new way, a way
more appropriate to today's world, including our growing understanding of
the universe and our recognition that we are all individual representations of
one Awareness, of *That Which Is,* by whatever name any of us choose to call it.

INTRODUCTION

Nothing in this book — or any book — is the answer.

You are the answer.

A new aspect of understanding, according to quantum physics, is that for as infinitely as the universe seems to expand outwardly, so too does it seem to expand inwardly. The deeper inward that science allows us to go, the more we see that, at the quantum level, there is mostly what science is fond of referring to as empty space—an apparent void of nothingness. At the same time, everything in the universe that ever was and ever will be is contained within this space, and it's all connected through a field beyond space and time. That space is consciousness and awareness. Yet not always in the way we *think* of consciousness and awareness.

It's this force (or *force field of perception*) that engenders life and awareness, holds our bodies together in form and matter, and gives structure to solar systems, galaxies, the universe, the multiverse and beyond. It's also through this field that a higher aspect of ourselves speaks to our human self. The intention of these whispers is to guide us toward greater degrees of wholeness, expression and purpose. One might refer to this as an *inner calling*. *We* call it Energy, Light & Information experiencing itself as each of us in finite space and time. Or, a receivership called the Reconnective Healing Experience.

Whether we're listening or not, or even if we choose to ignore the infinite whispers, we all receive inner callings at different points in our life. For some it's a whisper over a lifetime, for others it's a clap of thunder.

Reconnective Healing is *my* calling, and now that I teach it alongside my life partner, Jillian, it's *our* calling. The funny thing about a calling is that, while you may be called in many directions and in many ways, and while at times it may be physically, mentally and/or emotionally exhausting, in *answering* the call, you receive a different kind of strength and energy, one born out of service and love itself.

When you are introduced to something in the manner in which we were introduced to Reconnective Healing, you realize your calling is part of the larger design, the mission of which is to usher onto our planet this intelligence—Infinite intelligence. The result is evolutionizing humanity from attachment to knowledge back to an all *knowingness* that precedes all experiences and emerges as the experience of human *light* that each of us IS.

What we want you to know is that when the Reconnective Healing frequencies first became tangible in experience, a literal *portal* has opened up. It isn't so much a *visible* portal, but it is definitely a *literal* portal in that it began modulating into this dimension of height, width, depth and time, which we now understand as Energy, Light & Information®.

I could *feel IT*. I could *find IT*.

And *IT* found *me*.

So what *is IT* and how are we going to *explain IT* in this book? First of all, we are referring to an intelligence that is entirely different from *anything* we could have conceived of in our previously perceived 3D reality, a reality we considered as being composed of height, width and depth, the summation of which creates the space in which our body-mind lives.

Around the year 2000, however, when science finally accepted what Einstein had been telling us since the 1950s, time was acknowledged as the fourth dimension. By the very act of perceiving *IT* we've moved outside of our four-dimensional existence to become what is today referred to as *multidimensional*. Although technically anything beyond 1D is multidimensional, the use of the word "multidimensional" acknowledges the transition into nonlinear and has become the accepted designation. (There's also a lot to be said for the term *omnidimensional*.) It's fair to say too that the nature of this intelligence is to bring order, coherence and wholeness into being—in other words, *IT* brings order, coherence and wholeness into places and spaces where disorder, incoherence and division previously existed.

IT operates *in* us,
around us,
through us
and *as* us.
Rather than us *reaching out* to *IT*
We *receive.*
And the experience is our *reception of* and *return to* IT
a new language, in a sense,
entering into a silent understanding,
dissolving all sense expression.
Peace.
Your experience of It
is the healing.
No space-time.
Healing is our recognition that we are wholeness.
Always whole.
One entity.
Reconnected,
no longer dependent on the illusion of
"Separate self"
But rather, being
our purpose,
wholeness
as oneness,
and nothing less than that reception
defines us.

This is the Reconnective Healing Experience.

BEFORE YOU READ ANY FURTHER...

*Before you read any further, write down everything you feel, believe, know or think you may know, about healing... your thoughts, opinions, ideas, concepts, fear-based holdbacks and exciting drives forward. Return to what you've written as often as you like throughout the reading of this book and later on, when you read the book again. **Live a little: write in ink!** Feel free to add to what you've written, yet don't erase anything. At a later point if something in your notes no longer applies and you want to cross it out, place a single line through it so you have the option to revisit it and see where you once were. You will find yourself returning more than once, both while reading this book and afterward, to follow your progression. You will discover this to be a wonderful travel guide through your own evolution!* You will also discover that **you are integral to a process that is here in great scope.**

CHAPTER 1

THE GIFT OF THE HEALER

"We are ... an integral part of the world that we perceive; we are not external observers. We are situated within it. Our view of it is from within its midst. We are made up of the same atoms and the same light signals as are exchanged between pine trees in the mountains and stars in the galaxies."

—Carlo Rovelli

And Then Came Jered ...

Birthday gifts, holiday gifts and wedding presents are generally surprises. That's why we wrap them before giving them to the recipient. Let's face it, the excitement level is often at a peak while opening the package, whether gently unwrapping it to save the paper (which, between you and me, we'll never use again anyway) or rabidly tearing off the ribbon and ripping through the wrapping paper as if the gifts you didn't open yet might disappear if you don't open this one quickly enough! Healings, too, are surprises. The wrapping paper may not be from a department store, the contents may not be something preselected from a gift registry, yet the revealing of the gift comes at its own pace and rhythm. Nothing you can do to speed it up and no clue as to what's inside. Often you can't even figure out how the present fit into the packaging to begin with!

This was the case with Jered. ... Jered was only four when his mother brought him in to see me. With braces on his knees that would no longer hold him up and eyes that were gazing off in two directions at once yet unable to focus on any one thing, words no longer came from his mouth . . . and in the void was the endless flow of saliva. Jered's light had been reduced to a vacant expression that showed barely a glimmer of the beautiful being that dwelled within.

He had been losing the myelin coating of his brain on which nerve impulses travel, and as a result been suffering through approximately fifty grand mal seizures per day. Medication reduced the number of daily seizures to approximately sixteen.

As he lay there on the table, motionless and almost without expression, his mother explained that over the past year she had helplessly watched his rapid deterioration. By the time of her first visit with me, she found herself left not with the child she once knew, but with what she could only describe as "an amoeba."

During Jered's first session, whenever my hand would approach the left side of his head, he would sense its presence and reach for it. "Look! He knows where your hand is. He's reaching. He never does that," his mother pointed out with hopeful surprise. She took in a deep breath and added, "That's where the myelin is missing." Jered became so active that by the end of that session his mother had to sit by him on the table, lightly holding his hands, placatingly singing children's songs as only a mother can. Their favorite was "Twinkle, Twinkle, Little Star." The day of Jered's first session, his physically violent seizures stopped. Completely.

Jered's second session found him grasping at doorknobs and beginning to turn them. His vision improved, and he was now able to focus on objects. On his way out of the office, he pointed to a floral arrangement in our reception area: "Flowers," he said, smiling. There wasn't a dry eye in the room.

That night, Jered was discovered reciting the letters of the alphabet with a talk show host on a television game show. And before he went to sleep, this formerly speechless cherub looked up toward his mother and said, "Mommy, sing to me." Five weeks later, Jered was back at school. On the playground. Catching balls.

—Excerpted and edited from a story Eric wrote for a book
called *Hot Chocolate for the Mystical Soul*, compiled by
Arielle Ford

The gift of being invited into the RHE as the catalyst comes in the witnessing itself, and in the disappearance of otherness; the discovery of the infinite and eternal love that we are. And, once in a while, getting the opportunity in the middle of the day to sing "Twinkle, Twinkle, Little Star."

There seems to be a stigma in today's culture around healing, specifically around the people we call *healers*, and *the power we give away to them* consciously and not so consciously. The power we give away to them is *our own intrinsic power*. Oftentimes when we hear that someone is a healer, there's an automatic assumption that this person is somehow endowed with very particular, highly extraordinary characteristics, or that this person is somehow specially anointed by God with supernatural powers.

When you think about it in this way, it automatically sets the stage for the perceived illusion of the healer as something or someone being "more" in our eyes, which diminishes our recognition of ourselves by comparison. This only serves to create a hallucination of a chasm between ourselves and God, or, if you want to be a bit more agnostic about it, what philosophers and theologians ranging from Aristotle to St. Thomas Aquinas to Immanuel Kant described as "First Cause."

The history of mankind is the evolution of our ideas, and ideas exist at the intersection of our consciousness and the external world. One of the earliest ideas of our ancient ancestors was that they were more than just a body, and that when they disembodied upon death, they became spirits with the power to inhabit all things, from objects to places to creatures. This belief is called *animism*—the attribution of a spiritual essence or "soul" to all objects and beings, human and otherwise. The term *animism* comes from Latin, the root *anima* literally meaning "breath, spirit and life." Some scholars believe *animism* is likely to be humanity's earliest expression of anything that could be termed *religion*.

In 1989, a site called Ohalo II was discovered in Israel on the southwest shore of the Sea of Galilee, Lake Kinneret, near the city of Tiberias. It provided evidence that approximately 23,000 years ago we humans traded in our spears for plows and consequently transformed from foragers into farmers. The ensuing results of this transition were among the most significant developments in human history. As an agricultural-based society began to develop, including the domestication of animals, this pushed mankind further away from the idea that we were all connected. Instead of mankind being an indelible part of the earth, mankind now claimed dominion over it. And as the nomadic way of living gave way to societies, organized religions began to arise.

Originally created as a way to understand our place in the world and the universe, at times these religions created hierarchies as ways to maintain power. And so, after many millennia, the idea of *animism,* which was to say there was no distinction between the spiritual world and the physical world, gave way to the idea that God was something separate or outside of us.

Now that society was becoming restructured and hierarchies were emerging, how would a commoner get access to God? Well, if they wanted better access to God, they'd better go see their priest, priestess, shaman or holy man/woman.

As the ideas of man evolve, reorganize and modernize in accordance with our scientific discoveries, so too do many faiths. With the emergence of quantum physics and other scientific discoveries evidencing that we are all connected through a field of information, all of a sudden it seems like the idea of God being something separate from us has become quite antiquated. Instead, validation is emerging for the understanding that God is *in* us and we *are* God.

As a sidebar, because "God" can be such a divisive term for some, feel free to replace the word "God" with "Source," "Energy," "the Unified Field," "baklava," "tulip," "umbrella," "lutefisk" or whatever else you choose. It's essentially a word for *That Which Is,* which is why it's so hard to comprehend why so many humans *still* create wars in the name of this word.

Whether you're religious or don't practice a religion is not the point. Whether you believe in God or are an atheist is also not the point. The point is that just as mankind is rediscovering the idea that we are not separate from God, we are also evolving past the idea that only someone specially designated as a healer—while ascribing a special rare or unique attribute to that person—can bequeath a healing.

The new way means being a healer and the healing itself are not separate from us. We are both the healer *and* the healing. And in being so, we not only heal others, we also heal ourselves and, in the process, we heal the world. In being so, we bring light to ourselves, to others and to the world. This makes everyone special *and no one special*! The supernatural can be thus recognized as what it always truly has been: *super-natural*. And the extraordinary can now be recognized as what *it* has always been: *extra-ordinary*. And all of us can finally *just get real*.

Everyone Is Special and No One Is Special

Reconnective Healing is not a religion, nor is it of any one religion. RH respects all religions and recognizes that in the great many spiritual paths of the world, great truths are to be found in all their writings. For example, depending on which New Testament translation you reference, in John 14:12 you will find that Jesus says, "These things I do, you shall do also…and greater." Or "The works that I do you will do also; and greater works than these you will do." And "You will do the same things I am doing. You will do even greater things…" On and on, you will find these teachings in virtually every translation. For many, this can be a challenging statement to accept. If the thought of doing what Jesus did doesn't intimidate you already, there are many who would try to disabuse you of that idea entirely. And often in the very name of the person who spoke those words himself—*Jesus*! What most of us don't realize is that we are far more powerful than we imagine.

Marianne Williamson, one of today's great spiritual teachers, frames it this way: "Our deepest fear is not that we are inadequate. Our deepest fear is that we are powerful beyond measure. It is our light, not our darkness, that most frightens us."

What some people fear, many to the point of not even allowing themselves to explore the meaning of these teachings, is that they may very well be powerful beyond measure, as Marianne and others tell us. Very often it's these same people who, as they see you living up to *your* potential, feel inadequate because they may not see themselves as living up to their own and fear that they may never do so. It's the price of living in comparison and judgment. Instead of a willingness to risk and attempt to attain their own success, they often resort to discrediting or disparaging those who do achieve success. This fear-based, passive-aggressive—sometimes actively aggressive—cowardice and bullying is known as the *Tall Poppy Syndrome*, which in summary means don't be the tallest poppy or you'll get your head chopped off to bring it down in line with the average. This is where we are challenged to transcend fear

5

and live in love—to live in our light, not our darkness. What all of this really comes down to is the issue of *worthiness*.

The Reconnective Healing Experience offers a level playing field where each and every one of us is the person who is delivered, anointed and endowed with the ability to heal—to be as tall a poppy as you want. This is the true nature of healing. Anything other than that is affectation, plain and simple. Because the healing is not *outside* of us, it is *within* us, and when we open ourselves up to be the catalyst, we *become* the healing. The healer in each of us is the true part of our nature that exists simultaneously before and beyond our physical humanity. In other words, everyone possesses the power to be a healer even though it's not as much a power as it is an inalienable right of our true essence and evolution.

The paradigm shift at play is that we are not moving *toward* wholeness, but rather we *are already* wholeness, and healings occur in this awakening and awareness. We only need to step *into* it. We may have lost our way from this essential truth, but this moment in history is about reclaiming that knowingness. In Reconnective Healing, *because* there is no hierarchy and no "chosen" person, it comes down to our recognition and the totality of our experiences choices, and within each of those exists levels of accountability.

The evolution of our humanity resides in our accountability to accept our role as healers for ourselves, others and the planet. Notice we said *accountability*, not *responsibility*. We point this out because there is an important distinction to be made between those two words. The main difference is that responsibility can be that of many while accountability is singular. Being accountable means being responsible for something and having to answer for it. What it comes down to, then, is that life lived from the perspective of knowing your true nature is a gift that you're accountable for, and to be accountable for your own life and well-being makes you accountable for *everyone's* life and well-being. That is the gift of true oneness, healing and life progress.

When a thought arises, carefully ask yourself, "Where did that thought come from?" You'll see then, that thoughts are not placed into awareness from the outside. There is no outside. No limit or border. There is only the totality of who we are—source consciousness manifest in physical embodiment. Some people are the embodiment of the healer their entire life. They are accountable for all aspects of their life and recognize that life is a gift and an evolution, that experience is a roadmap, that they make a difference, their choices in the present moment pave the way for future events, and that by their presence alone they are a healer. Others are not even accountable for the fact that they exist. They neither acknowledge nor have the presence of mind to realize that what happens in their life is part of a much larger chain of interactions. They seek external things to fill a void inside of them, rather than looking at what that void within them really requires to be filled.

In this example, if we refine this down to its most simple elements, there may only be but two paradigms for the thinking mind: that we live in a connected universe where everything is interrelated; or that we live in a separate and distinct universe—a disconnected universe in which everything is random and arbitrary.

One paradigm recognizes a person as accountable for their life and their healing, as well as the healing of the planet and everyone who exists on it, the other does not. One is a *we* world and the other is a *me* world. In which paradigm would you rather live? Our guess is, if you're reading this, it's the former.

The Simplicity in Healing

> *"Something is elegant if it is two things at once: unusually simple and surprisingly powerful."*
>
> —*Matthew E. May*

In healing, simplicity is an opportunity that exists without the feeling or need to introduce enhancements or safeguards. The healer functions in presence, requiring no additions or enhancements. The healer realizes that in the very presence of these intended enhancements and safeguards, healing is reduced, or possibly ceases to exist altogether.

In Reconnective Healing, there is no need for rituals, techniques, healing tools or trinkets, protections, intentions, visualizations, memorizations, etc. These only obscure the purity of the healer, which is revealed when we transcend our reliance on these, the externals. It is revealed when all else falls away and the inner compass of knowingness, in authenticity and truth, arises from within you, allowing you to genuinely recognize that *you are enough*. You exist, you observe, you witness, you dissolve otherness. In this recognition of receiving you catalytically inspire the healee into consciousness' infinite potential, while simultaneously recognizing your own.

Receive. Reception. No need to try to *send* healing, just receive healing. The very thought or attempt to send instills a concept of distance, a false sense of separation or division which, at best, dilutes and further obscures healing, simultaneously plunging you into an *otherness* that, at a very base level, and generally not even a cognizant one, instills a sense of sadness and fear. It therefore subliminally seeks temporary satisfaction by soothing the ego through rituals, protections and states that further reinforce the cycling of *more* feelings of separation, *more* fear and *more* cravings to soothe.

In receiving, you step into unity, your own transfiguration and intimacy as the pure sensation of infinite intelligence that dissolves the content of experience that's been veiling the perfection of your oneness, your transformation, *you*. It is here you are a receiving device, a sort of *Bluetooth, pairable as Source-Intelligence,* available to pair with another and dissolve the otherness. You become a participant and agent for healing, allowing everyone to step into their own healing equation, perfectly designed for them. And thus you're both introduced to the true art of reception without the need to send, oneness without the need to fabricate otherness, love without the empty illusion of fear and separation. This is what it means to be a healer. This is the Reconnective Healing Experience.

What makes simplicity so complex?

Complexity by its very definition means something that's difficult to understand or conceptually grasp. So why is simplicity such a seemingly complex achievement? Because in most cases, it is a reduction of elements that we've grown attached to, content creations we were told we needed that were never needed in the first place. They were merely the imagined needs of the people who brought us these ideas. They were *their* superstitions and attachments that for multiple reasons we bought into and that brought us a false sense of comfort and security. And because of that attachment, we're simply afraid of what we *think* we might have to give up to attain what simply *is*.

If we're willing, however, to give up our attachments to certain ideas and things we *believe* keep us safe and secure, things that feel *familiar* or that we consider *authoritative* or *right,* then in the vacated space of these attachments new ideas, concepts and energy can flow. In reality, we give up very little, if *anything,* to gain so much.

What this comes down to is that we have to be willing to give up the illusion that we need something outside of us to produce a healing. Could it perhaps be that the illusion is an aberration, an apparition, a fantasy, something we are hiding behind because we are in fact fearful of the *potentiality* of our innate, divine power to both heal ourselves and be a healer of others?

At the core of Reconnective Healing, simplicity is a letting go of our attachment to techniques, including those techniques intrinsic to our many known modalities, a releasing of our hopes and beliefs in external objects to give us special powers, protections, special *anythings,* or, dare we say, anything that we believe will make us "more" in any way.

When all this falls away, all that remains is our communion with the IS. The conduit, igniting us, igniting *you,* the explorer, facilitator/healer into receivership. Through this you become the newly inspired catalyst for healing. Everything else is merely clutter and illusion, obscuring the beauty and simplicity of the Before-Beyond, Source, truth, freedom, love, presence. The ever-presence that is *you.*

Presence is key because it intersects with timelessness, which is at once a seeming paradox; an inverse of our understanding, a bit of a conundrum for many, to say the least.

In this space,
what falls away is the distraction,
what remains is the attraction.
What falls away is the external,
what remains is the internal.
What falls away is the temporal,
what remains is the eternal.
What falls away is the illusion,
what remains is the reality.
What falls away is the lie,
what remains is the veracity.
What falls away is the suit of armor,
what remains is the attention of the heart.

We all enjoy a little mystery, a little mystique every once in a while. It's alluring, it's enticing. Yet in the healing field, it's easy to suddenly find ourselves more than a bit lost in a cycle of self-perpetuating, indeterminate mystique, the seemingly endless and secretively complex unknown. The mystique itself may make us feel separate and unique. The techniques allow us to feel masterful and in control. And the rituals may make us feel as if we're part of an elite group, lineage or tradition. The protections might even make us feel as if we're playing with something dangerous and powerful, while all they really do is keep us in a fear-based dynamic.

All of this is part of a seductive and addictive cycle, down to sometimes even the way we feel this allows us to appear in the eyes of others; a way that gives us short bursts of superficial pleasure, though nonsustaining because they're based on the temporal.

Truly, the Reconnective Healing Experience *is* its own reward. To get there, we have to embrace our *own* truth and be all we are! Not necessarily what we *desire* our truth to be—not what we may outwardly *insist upon* or *cling to* as our own truth—but the truth that speaks when we quietly ask *ourselves* who we are, what our truth really is. That truth is the voice that whispers in the silence when there's no-thing and no-one but you present to hear the answer.

Healing. It's such a beautiful word. And yet it's very utterance can ignite a maelstrom of responses and reactions that head straight into the emotional. And not always are these the prettiest of emotions. The word seems to elicit one of two responses: either *fear,* often loud and voluminous, pretty much screaming for attention, or *love.* Very rarely does there appear to be any middle ground.

Agreeing to redefine this word, as well as expanding the understanding of our essential and fundamental relationship to the inherent simplicity that *is* healing, may well be the lost jewel that allows humanity to reach its God-given potential.

The elegance of the healer, in both form and formless, in both movement and rest, is a receivership from which the healing arises out of stepping into loving detachment. In this pure reception you release your attachment both to the person receiving the healing as well as to the healing outcome. Once we gain this insight, we find ourselves on a path from which there is little desire to or satisfaction in turning back.

So there is the *elegant simplicity* and there is the *grace* of the healer, a non-judgment that encompasses all involved.

The nonjudgment comes from there being no determinations around whether or not the healing experience was good, bad, better or indifferent relative to whether or not the desired outcome was attained. Instead, there is the realization that every healing is perfection and that our own healing grows from our ever-expanding recognition and knowing that each time is *exactly* what we need—whether that's something tangible and nameable, wanted or unwanted, or that occurs at a much deeper level of our essence. Our *own* healing is directly related to our ability to recognize the perfection in each person's healing, including our own.

You might think that to be a catalyst for an optimal healing, you have to be in a "state of love," ideally one that you are cognizant of, appreciative and grateful for. Beautiful as that may sound, this is *not* a requirement because we are Love irreducibly, whether or not we are experiencing it in a cognizant state. "Love" is a word in healing that conjures up as many varied interpretations as there are clouds in the sky. It's not about being in a *state* of love—it's about *being love itself.* It's not about *thinking* love, *wishing* love upon the person on your healing table and so on. Instead, you investigate the I that is *love itself,* because *love is*—think of the metaphor of one candle lighting another candle, or two hearts becoming one, or two biophotons entraining—what is created is an infinite, indistinguishable Reconnective Healing Experience where there is no longer separation. No separation. *None.*

While we don't know what the healing is going to amount to for the receiver you pair with, your presence as the witness is the *catalyst* for the healing. Your presence allows you to actually witness, with awe and wonder, healing being bestowed in this equation with the pure lovingness of shared being and without the need or even the desire to know the details of how or why.

In Reconnective Healing, this is both a significant part of the healing equation and a significant part of what it means to be the healer.

In exploring our receptivity as Energy, Light & Information—God, Love and Infinite Intelligence—true love reveals itself as our reality. Although you may not always be conscious of it, you express yourself as this infinite reconnected being and pure awareness. This is your role in existence as consciousness made manifest. Existence itself! We can easily confuse the word "existence" with "being." *Being* is the background from which all things emerge. Existence, or the Latin *existere,* means to stand forth, come out, emerge, appear to be visible, come to light. This is your role as the healer—to make simple what appears to be a constellation of infinite potentials and possibilities. To make the unknowable knowable, the intangible tangible, the inaccessible accessible and the incomprehensible comprehensible.

Let's pause and take note of a few things we've already explored:

We reviewed some integral concepts such as our lives being in a connected universe; the elegance in healing being its simplicity; and awareness superseding the need for ritual, technique, protection, intention and healing objects. We also discovered that we're receivers functioning as Bluetooths, pairable with everyone and everything; that the grace of the healer is nonjudgmental communion with the Reconnective Healing Intelligence and, ultimately, that it's not about *thinking* love, it's not about *wishing* love, it's purely about *being love itself!*

In summation, being a healer is a gift that may only be received, only be experienced, when we are no longer looking to add or supplement. And only when we are no longer looking to add or supplement may we truly be the healer. We are at once the healer, the healee *and* the healing.

This is a wonderful spot for us to change pace a bit and pivot into the first of our interactive exercises.

Exercise 1:
Painting Your Palm with the Frequencies:
An Exploration into Receiving

While you're sitting at home or someplace where you can allow yourself to relax, open your left hand and hold it perpendicular to the ground. Now spread the fingers of your left hand open somewhat widely and *look into your left palm.* While you are looking into your left palm, bring your *right* hand up by the side of your head with the fingers of your right hand also open and spread fairly wide. Remember, keep staring at your left palm and watch the fingers of your left hand while keeping the fingers of both hands spread wide open, maintaining a little bit of a *pulling sensation,* a *slight* tension in the muscles of your palms.

Imagine that the skin of your left palm is a canvas stretched tightly, ready for an artist to begin painting, and that the surface of your right palm is spreading or spraying paint onto that canvas. Keep a slight tension in each of your hands as you gently glide your right hand up and down slowly, easily, allowing yourself to *feel anything you happen to feel,* even if it's just the feeling of the air as your palm glides through it. Feel free to start at a distance anywhere from three inches to three feet (7.5–90 cm). We would suggest starting at about a one-foot (30 cm) distance and then expanding outward. Truly, the only guidepost or limitation to this distance is your physical or emotional comfort level, which will expand as you allow it. Remember that *feeling is listening with a different sense.* And both *feeling* and *listening* are activities of *receiving* .

As you allow yourself to continue to glide your right hand while you observe your left hand, you may well begin to detect variations in *intensity, character* and *quality* of sensation, maybe first in one hand and then in the other. You might notice a temperature change or a fluctuation in vibration or resonance. You may well then even begin to observe movement in one or more of the fingers of your left hand, and possibly even in your right hand. Just observe, notice, explore different movements. Keep your eyes open. Maybe wiggle the fingers of your right hand a little. How does that affect the fingers of your left hand? If you're not sure at first, play for another few seconds and see what reveals itself to you. For variation, you may choose to gently employ a suction-like pumping motion from the center of your right hand. What changes does that bring about for you?

Allow yourself to *be* focus instead of trying to *maintain* focus. Free from effort, allow the petals of this flower to naturally unfold and reveal their beauty. As you play, as you paint, as you metaphorically dance with these frequencies, observe the animated expression of life in your hands and explore the sensorial manifestation. And feel free to email us about your experience with this and the other exercises that are coming up later in other chapters. We really do want to hear from you!

1. What did I learn from this chapter?
2. What did I discover from this exercise?
3. What ideas are new to me?
4. What ideas are different than I might have thought?
5. What ideas am I now considering, contemplating?
6. Which ideas feel the most natural to me?
7. Which ideas or concepts do I have the most difficulty with or find the greatest challenge in accepting?
8. Which ideas or concepts do I have the most difficulty with or find the greatest challenge in understanding?
9. Which of my previous beliefs and ideas do I find the greatest challenge in releasing and letting go of?
10. Which ideas and concepts do I find the most freeing and empowering?
11. What has my willingness to not know already allowed me to discover? To become?
12. What might my present willingness to not know allow me to discover in the future? To become?

Please respond to the above with your thoughts, possible answers, explanations, ideas, etc., to the best of your ability.

If you don't know how to answer some of the questions above or just don't have the words, we've designed a fill-in-the-blanks model below to help you.

1. I'm not sure I know, but if I did know, the answer might be _____

2. I don't quite have the words to explain this, but if I did have the words, they might be _____

3. I don't quite have the words to describe this, but if I did have the words, they might be_____

CHAPTER 2

THE GIFT OF ENERGY, LIGHT & INFORMATION

"If you want to find the secrets of the universe, think in terms of energy, frequency and vibration."

—*Nikola Tesla*

The Before-Beyond Measurement

The concept of *beyond* is an interesting and varied one. Something could be just beyond reach, someone could stay beyond his/her welcome. What we find especially interesting is when something is beyond an accepted standard. Meaning when we have to reevaluate our norms, measurements, understandings, perceptions and perhaps most especially our comfort zones.

When we are open to new ideas, it's in this place of openness and reevaluation where we are able to explore and unearth our own limitations and obscurations—self-imposed limitations based in egocentricity. Did you ever notice how the discussion of ego, or simply the *mention* of the word ego, brings up so much resistance and ... uh ... what's the word we're looking for here ... oh, yeah ... *ego!*

Why do we bring this up? Because the Reconnective Healing Experience allows us to exist and function *outside* the realm of ego, prior to, *before-beyond* the obscuration of ego, in *dissolution* of the ego. Ego simply is absent in the Reconnective Healing Experience. These frequencies exist in a realm that science today isn't capable of comprehensively measuring. How then do these frequencies fit within the spectrum of all frequencies?

Among other forms of assessment, science measures frequencies in kilo-hertz, megahertz and gigahertz with so much detail that, for the unscientific mind, this whole concept kinda hurts! Frequencies exist on mechanical waves and electromagnetic waves, such as microwaves, radio waves, sound waves and light waves—the jury's still out on permanent hair waves :)

A defining characteristic of electromagnetic waves is that they always travel at the same speed. The actual waves are measured in wavelengths, which are further broken down into frequency band charts based on timed intervals, and on and on and on.

From the time the Reconnective Healing frequencies made their debut, our human nature led us to attempt to classify them *within* something, within something that's already known. Staying inside our comfort zone is a human default. Yet if certain people throughout history never challenged the conventions of that zone, we'd still be living in the Stone Age. When we can't associate the unknown with something we already know and feel, something we're already familiar with, fear or awe generally happens. Fear of something that isn't clear, transparent or easily knowable through our mind's eye, or awe of the unknown in which multidimensionality is ignited and made manifest.

Maybe we eventually come to secretly acknowledge the existence of some-thing new, something not previously seen by us or believed at large. Yet, to be accepted by the majority, one strategy might be to suppress the truth and attempt to hide or deflect criticism by persecuting others who espouse what we secretly recognize to be true.

As longtime friend Lee Carroll, author of the *Kryon* books, explains: "There's a change of pace overall. With the advent of the Internet, there's a quickening. And there's a quickening in healing as well."

Reconnective Healing is that quickening.

By our very nature, we're eager to find a way to grasp, understand and describe what these frequencies of Energy, Light & Information are. We want to find a way to designate *IT* with a defined beginning, middle and end.

"What you are basically, deep, deep down, far, far in, is simply the fabric and structure of existence itself."

—Alan Watts

In our desperate search for comprehension, we try to discover *ITS* parameters. How does *IT* fit within given religious parameters or yogic and other practice parameters? Can *IT* be explained by or contained within existing philosophies and traditions? In other words, we want *IT* to fit neatly, cleanly and efficiently within our understanding of something, *anything*, based upon the *already known*. This gives us a sense of familiarity, comfort and security validating the world as we know it. Yet if we try to fit everything within what is *already known,* how will we ever discover *all that is unknown?*

If William Herschel had insisted that all color, or the perception of color, fits within the known wavelengths of light, he would never have discovered infrared light in 1800, nor would Johann Ritter have discovered ultraviolet light in 1801. Only when we're willing to entertain the possibility that *something* exists *beyond (and prior to)* our perceived parameters, and look *outside* of those perceived parameters, can we actually discover *what* exists *clear of* those parameters.

Which brings a related question: Can we allow ourselves to move beyond the ego, the perceiving part of the self that would have us believe we already know everything, and enter into the egoless, where we are open to pure discovery without judgment?

For many, this initially will require a change and an open awareness to new modes of thinking and of gathering information.

The Copernican Revolution is a great example of a radical change in thinking brought about through the discovery process. In the early part of the sixteenth century, Nicolaus Copernicus argued that the cosmos was composed of a different physical reality than that widely believed at the time. He shifted the paradigm from the Ptolemaic model of the heavens to the Heliocentric model, meaning the earth was no longer considered to be the center of the universe, but rather the sun was understood to be at the center, with the earth, the other planets and the stars orbiting around the sun. The Church, and therefore a lot of people, didn't want to accept this model. But eventually science proved it incontrovertible and today no one gives this a second thought.

Ironically, the majority of the public follows the lead of science, not aware that science follows the lead of those who don't wait. As Dr. Joe Dispenza says, "If we wait for science to give us an OK, we make it another religion. If we just go out and do it, then science has to change its laws to explain it."

It is unquestionably clear that Reconnective Healing parameters also cannot be found or quantified by present-day methods, if by any. That's because they simply don't fit within the boundaries, limitations or endpoints of any of our known scales. Unless and until we discover ways of measuring *far* greater parameters than the ones we are aware of, it will be difficult, if not impossible, to scientifically measure the breadth and scope of Reconnective Healing for what it is: Energy, Light & Information that is UTTERLY INFINITE INTIMACY.

In other words, although science is still attempting to catch up to what *is*—and for a very long time, if not forever, will continue to do so—at the very least, science is recognizing that the Energy, Light & Information that is Reconnective Healing *IS:* it *exists* even if science can't fully gauge, articulate or categorize it exactly. According to our current understanding of the laws of the universe, it just doesn't fit into any known taxonomy, hierarchy or healer's *toolbox.* It is borderless.

When Reconnective Healing first showed up here on earth, it came through a portal that suddenly *appeared and made itself known.* And through this portal came aspects and frequencies of Light and Information that I, Eric, and the research world, would come to understand more and more. For me to do this, I had to learn to truly observe. And I had to learn to observe from a different place and space than I had been used to. To observe without assigning meaning or interpretation, to be as pure as possible, is a challenge to the finite body-mind. And it certainly was for mine.

I didn't come from a seemingly conscious background that would allow me to understand *IT*s consistency, characteristics and qualities, although I must have come from a background that gave me at least some of the instinct I would need to draw upon.

It didn't take long to discover that when we engage with IT, we become the highest form of consciousness on the planet. Maybe not on a cognizant level, yet as our essential essence. And that's enough. More than enough. That's all *IT* is looking for. *IT* simply wants us to *observe, notice* and *experience*. And, at the same time, *IT* is here to experience itself *through* and *as us!* As Herschel and Ritter showed us, there's far more than meets the eye. And today such prominent names as neuroscientist and author Bernardo Kastrup and theoretical physicist and author Carlo Rovelli, join the distinguished ranks of those bringing ongoing insight to the recognition of the infinite.

Once we grasp this reality, we begin to understand why Reconnective Healing, which is infinite Energy, Light & Information, is not another tool for our healing toolbox. It can't be. Because it's not a tool at all. *Any* box, *any* tool, any *thing* is finite, limited by its very design. And all that is finite is encompassed within the infinite.

This means freedom and expansion. Once we access Reconnective Healing, we gain access to the *limitless,* access to our infinite self.

What allows us to access the limitless is the same thing that allowed Herschel and Ritter to discover infrared and ultraviolet light—a willingness to freely, simply and naturally self-inquire and explore our actual experience. In truth, that's all the understanding we need to remove our blinders so that we may see beyond the greater reaches, edges, spectrums and bandwidths of what we currently perceive as reality.

Think about the blinders on a racehorse for a moment. All the horse can see is what's in front of them. That limitation may help the horse win the race by limiting visual distractions (therefore financially benefiting the horse's owner), but it does so by severely limiting the horse's ability to see what's actually around them, as well as their ability to perceive that they, like us, are running on a greater track.

The Energy, Light & Information that is Reconnective Healing, being infinite in measure, is clearly beyond what we can metaphorically see with our own finite blinders on. But it is also the Reconnective Healing Experience that removes these blinders, granting us greater vision, insight and access to our infinite potential. The racehorse blinders model is a construct to show the ease and immediate accessibility for each and every one of us.

Once we realize and accept our nature as infinite beings, or, more accurately, infinite *being* or one Entity, one Consciousness, a new awakening for humanity will unfold. It's likely that this is the very reason we're living in history's most exciting moment to date, for it's only been in the last decade or so that science has strongly begun to make more accurately measurable the understanding that we are all connected, that we are all one. And by science demonstrating this, it's allowed a lot of us to remove our own blinders and begin to explore what we may not have given ourselves permission to explore up until now.

American philosopher and psychologist William James (also known as the Father of American Psychology) started down this road of us all being connected through a field of frequencies in his 1902 book, *The Varieties of Religious Experience.* James discovered that no matter what type of mystical experience a person had, even if the religious underpinnings were removed, the experience was more than psychologically real. He identifies a "noetic quality" and "states of insight into the depths of truth unplumbed by the discursive intellect."

This idea, however, was temporarily derailed by Sigmund Freud, the Austrian neurologist and founder of psychoanalysis. Freud was a devout atheist and didn't believe it was psychology's job to explore these states. He believed its purpose was to cure pathological problems. This idea was upended in the 1950s by Wilder Penfield, a neuroscientist and epilepsy expert. In performing epilepsy research, Penfield began applying a mild electrical probe to various parts of the brain. When he applied the electricity to the temporoparietal junction, he noticed people began having mystical encounters such as out-of-body experiences, near-death experiences and sensings of the presence of ghosts or even God. Experiences that were *biologically real*, which underscore the importance of this discovery.

And here we are today, not so much at a crossroads of science and spirituality, but with the understanding that with Reconnective Healing we enter into the long overdue recognition of the confluence of the two. It's for this reason that our friend and colleague Dr. Joe Dispenza says, "Science is the contemporary language of mysticism." Although ironically enough mainstream humanity started down this path more than 100 years ago, the idea has been widely overlooked in deference to Freud's psychological concepts.

Imagine where we might be today if for the past 100+ years we had lived with the understanding that everyone and everything is interconnected, *evolutionizing* humanity's finite experience into the greater expression of oneness and wholeness. Because we are all interconnected through the experience of consciousness, when we become adept in this recognition that our true nature resides outside of space and time, before all known experience, we can bring the fullness of our being to all active time/space experiences and *affect* this finite space and time with pure beauty, love, joy and happiness which, of course, affects *all* of space and time—not just the present, but what is perceived as the past and the future as well!

Before Words and Language

An interesting exploration of the power of nonverbal communication is Malcolm Gladwell's insightful book *Blink: The Power of Thinking Without Thinking* (2005). Investigating how we make many decisions in our life based on very little conscious information, Gladwell argues that many of these decisions are based upon nonverbal communication, body language, tone, facial expression and more. Only a small percentage of the communication is actually verbal, which means a greater part of the decision-making process comes from our subconscious.

We could call this information from the subconscious *instinct:* a knowingness that exists beyond our basic five senses. We would rephrase this common understanding to one of a knowingness that exists prior to or, as an accommodation to the limitation of language, *before* our basic five senses.

So let's get a bit metaphysical for a moment—a bit existential or spiritual. In the well-documented world of Near-Death Experiences (NDEs; also known as Life After Death Experiences), it's very common for people who experience an NDE to report highly detailed, in-depth communications occurring in the absence of verbal language. These transmissions (or downloads) are as voluminous as they are instantaneous. They range from copious amounts of information being transmitted by just a look or a glance between them and other souls who had passed and are present, to nonverbal communications shared with The Light including what are termed *Life Reviews,* the ability to review one's life instantaneously … although it may not feel so instantaneous at that moment.

Back here on earth, if we overlay that type of high-level, instantaneous communication with our verbal language, it would be fair to say that our vocabulary may not be so much an *assistance* to this type of communication as a *barrier* to it. If you agree with the idea that life here on earth is an unfolding journey of learning—a journey back to our greater understanding of our true nature and the experience of the universe—perhaps spoken language and communication may actually be one of the hurdles we are given to overcome in the mastery of life.

Perhaps language itself is the hurdle disguised as the assistance. Perhaps stepping beyond the complexity of words and language and into the comprehensive simplicity of the nonverbal is where our lessons and essential understandings are revealed.

This raises the question: Is spoken language the toolbox? Are facial expressions, body language, signs and symbols, vocal tones, etc., simply tools within that toolbox? Or is spoken language just one more tool among all of these? And has the entirety of the communication we've been having here merely been part of a much larger, dare we say infinite, field of communication, one that we are not consciously privy to here in our 4D human existence, our finite body-mind?

To begin with, we find information in *everything, everyone* and *everywhere.* Information is what allows the things in our physical realities to have and maintain certain properties such as strength, pliability, rigidity, overall form and structure as well as interactivity and intra-activity. Information instructs the functions of certain elements to exist as a solid, liquid or gas. From the macro to the micro, information instructs everything from the structure of the universe to the functionalities of our cells to that of subatomic particles. And we already know that the majority of our communication of all this information is nonverbal in nature. And it is now commonly understood by science that these nonverbal communications exist in a field referred to, from a materialist perspective, as consciousness. In the direct path to healing this is quite paradoxical because consciousness is not a "thing," it isn't a noun and inserting "-ness" at the end of the word "conscious" implies that it is. And therein lies the linguistic paradox.

Conversations with the Light:
A Sharing by Joan Fowler,
Reconnective Healing Practitioner

"A glance, a gesture, a tilt of the head conveys volumes."

Every NDE is different ... but many have similarities, and one of the similarities that are experienced in an NDE is nonverbal communication.

I'd like to share with you my NDE (Near-Death Experience) which occurred in 1989 at the age of 29. As I was cycling down Pacific Coast Highway when I was unexpectedly hit by a truck from the side. I found myself floating 20 to 30 feet above my body which, physically, was partially under the truck. I was not in pain. I was just curiously observing the crowd as I floated above it. I watched as people circled around me and I could hear their thoughts. It was as if nothing was hidden and I had the ability to see the life and thoughts of any of the onlookers that I focused on.

I could hear three distinct groups of thoughts from the crowd. In the first group, people wanted to help but didn't know what to do. In the second group, people wanted to help but were afraid of being sued. And the third group of people were just curious. I could also hear the ambulance gently whirring in the distance. Toward my right side I felt a magnetic presence of love and peace. As I turned my focus toward this beautiful, palpable and joyful light, I started to merge with it. It was as if my boundary conditions of physicality, of this existence, were dropping or fading away.

As I more fully merged with the light, I could feel myself in every molecule of water, in every blade of grass, in all the trees, in the universe ... There was nowhere that I was not. There was no separation, everything was known and experienced simultaneously. I could hear a whooshing and humming sound in the background. The answers to any BIG questions that I had about life, about our existence, etc., came to me before I could even formulate the question! I was experiencing immense peace and ecstatic joy simultaneously. I thought this is so wondrous, I could stay here forever. Immediately I heard or felt a knowingness convey to me: "Yes, you can stay," implying I had a choice ... "but what about your mother and grandmother?"

In that instant a vortex opened and my focus moved toward it. I was immediately drawn in. At the very end of the vortex I saw the ambulance which had my body in it. My awareness swirled into the vortex and emerged in the ambulance where I saw a very stressed EMT sweating and hovering over me, panicked and worried. As I focused on him, I could feel his life, I could see his two younger daughters and could feel the love he had for them and his wife. I could also see that morning he had made homemade banana pancakes for them. I could actually smell them, and in that scented instant, I was back in my body. He was so relieved and said, "Whew ... we almost lost you!"

For a while after the accident, I still had a sensation of expanded awareness where I could feel how people were doing in their life. I was also having revelatory dreams that communicated depth of being. I tried to explain to my parents that I was having these experiences and they attributed it to the fact that I wasn't wearing a helmet that day and must have experienced a concussion. They encouraged me to have a brain scan.

It took a while to recover as my shoulder needed to be reconstructed and reattached. Very near the end of recovery I was reactivated in the Army Reserve for active duty, and became averse to saying anything about the accident or its aftermath for obvious reasons. I always trusted the experience as true and understood it as a revelation on some level.

Almost 20 years after my NDE I picked up the book The Reconnection: Heal Others, Heal Yourself.

Immediately I experienced a strong electrical current in my hands, head and spine. I knew I needed to pay attention. The book seemed so familiar ... it was so clearly true.

I eventually scheduled several Reconnective Healing Experience sessions in which I found myself having the same sensations as in my near-death experience, incredible peace and joy beyond description and so much more. More information, more understanding. Again the communication was ineffable and beyond words, but the meaning was clear: we are love, we are light and this is our birthright. I began to more fully understand the depth of the experience 20 years prior and was elated to have confirmation it was real. Over my next few Reconnective Healing Experiences, I felt all my questions were answered.

The RH Experience brought balance to my life and helped me to fully integrate my NDE and awaken to an ever-expanding universe of possibilities. I now see that this expanded awareness is essential to our evolution as a species and it is essential to our interconnectedness and discernment in worlds to come. It brings with it the wisdom of the ages, the wisdom of lifetimes and multiple existences.

Why am I sharing my experience?
I found out that statistically 400 people per second around the world are having NDEs, STEs (spiritually-transformative experiences), OBEs (out-of-body experiences) and other transformative experiences during which intensely meaningful and insightful communications take place without words. Reconnective Healing brings context and understanding to these extraordinary experiences assisting with the integration of knowingness and expanded awareness on many levels. Energy, Light & Information are the frequencies of home, they are recognized and remembered intrinsically.

This common experience of love and oneness binds us to each other on infinite levels. It is a nonverbal communique, a wordless language of "being" that awakens us to infinite awareness, imbues us with balance and harmony. As we awaken to our truth, our life becomes Magical Wonder.

Consciousness exists in a relativistic way. Meaning you can access what you are vibrationally in alignment with or in tune with. We are all part of a collective consciousness of ONE with multiple focuses.

Communication with the Other Side? There is no "other side." There is only frequency and vibration . . . LOVE.

Time Balloons and Multidimensionality

Within the paradigm of today's world of quantum physics, we are in a time of what some call *information medicine*, or, more accurately, *information **healing.*** Information healing is far more apropos because the concept has much less to do with medicine than with the bigger picture of healing. As the world is coming to recognize, although medicine may fall within the realm of healing, healing is not conscribed to or within the realm of medicine. A great shift of awareness is underway, though that has brought us far beyond the limitations of the chemical and surgical approach to health, far beyond what was considered the energetic approach, and into more of an informational approach to health. Light and information, to be more accurate. The Reconnective Healing Experience through the frequencies of Energy, Light & Information to be precise.

As researchers began to study Reconnective Healing, they started by taking measurements of the emanations flowing and radiating from Eric's hands and, soon after, from the hands of our students. While observing these unusual emissions, the researchers were surprised to notice that the emanations became *stronger with distance* rather than weaker, as they had expected since we know that energy becomes weaker with distance. They also noted that most of these healings were immediate and didn't weaken over time, making it clear that they were observing aspects of light and information they had never before been seen.

One researcher explained, which is our own explanation as well, that we all live in a vast multidimensional universe that has no beginning and no end, not in time and not in distance or space. As flesh-and-blood human beings, however, we occupy a tiny sliver of this multidimensional spectrum of reality, suggesting that our physicality only exists within the four dimensions of height, width, depth and time.

As we mentioned earlier, it was only around the year 2000 when science finally accepted Einstein's theory that time is the fourth dimension. Perhaps part of why it took so long to accept this was the assumption that if height appeared as high, low, tall or short, and width appeared as wide or narrow, and depth appeared as deep or shallow, the next dimension would have similar qualities to the first three. But they weren't looking for *time*! How could they? No one really knew what time *looked* like. Really, who would think, *"Hmm, the fourth dimension ... ? OK, let me think ... height looks like this, width looks like that, depth looks like the other and ... umm ... Oh, I've got it! ... The fourth dimension must look like an old man with a beard, wings and a robe, carrying a scythe in one hand, an hourglass in the other and appearing frighteningly similar to Father Time (or, for some, the Grim Reaper!). This is certain to get me a Nobel Prize!"*

Putting mathematics aside, along with questionable taste in clothing and accoutrements, at first glance time appeared to be a characteristic of the physical world unlike anything that exists in height, width and depth. That alone took some getting used to. So how does time relate to us in the here and now, nonetheless how we thought it might have related to us in the linear perspective of the there and then? A friend who is a quantum physicist simplified the concept with a new model.

To understand this model, visualize a huge, vast, endless multidimensional universe. No beginning. No end. Then, somewhere within it, imagine a giant balloon. The balloon is comprised of height, width, depth and time, and everything within that balloon is energy. The interior of this balloon represents our perceived, four-dimensional universe. In other words, all of our four-dimensional human existence is contained within that balloon.

Now to stretch your imagination—and our balloon—imagine a dot. Imagine it right there, smack center in the middle of that balloon. From that central point, imagine rubber-tipped arrows (so the balloon doesn't pop) flying continuously outward in all directions toward the inner lining of the balloon. These arrows signify time simultaneously moving and accelerating in all directions. We know what you're thinking: How can we say time is accelerating or moving faster when *faster* is actually an aspect of time? First, we need to understand that time is not moving faster in a linear fashion, as in from point A to point B. Instead, time is moving faster in all conceivable directions—*all at once.*

So, in this visual or pictorial metaphor, imagine these arrows of speeding time creating an increasing pressure as each one touches the interior of our balloon, resulting in its ever-increasing expansion.

As with any balloon that expands, its walls become thinner, more sheer, more permeable and more porous. As a result, what existed inside our four-dimensional balloon is now able to interact with what exists outside of it. So, what exists *outside* of the balloon that is now able to *permeate* the inside? The answer according to the researchers: *other dimensional layers that contain aspects of light and information that up until the last 30 years science didn't seem to indicate we've ever before witnessed.* Why is this so? Because these aspects of light and information only existed *outside* of this bubble, outside of *time, in the Before-Beyond.* So the energy of our four-dimensional existence is now expanding into, receiving and interacting with not just new aspects of energy, but with new aspects and frequencies of light and information. *Timeless* because they've *always existed* outside of our four-dimensional bubble of height, width, depth and time. Yet *new* because this is their first appearance inside this metaphorical bubble.

This is both powerful and noteworthy because it is guiding us into our existence as timeless beings. It's releasing us from the requirements and limitations of *doing,* and bringing us into the freedom of *being,* a freedom many of us are just now learning to experience, just now beginning to feel comfortable enough to embrace. There's no way of making sense of this with the standard laws of physics, though quantum physics is striving to make further inroads into explaining it.

Let's revisit what we just explained:

    A. Time is moving faster, which means,

    B. Time is expanding, leading us to the fact that,

    C. Time is disappearing, which ultimately leads us to the realization that,

    D. Time is, and has always been, an illusion.

Intrigued? So were we. Here's where we get into a few interesting twists and turns.

If the universe is expanding in this fashion, why are we *not* able to access it through our current and accepted energy healing techniques, yet we *are* able to access it through the Reconnective Healing Experience *as we let go of technique?* To answer that, let's once again visualize our balloon.

Remember, everything within our four-dimensional balloon is energy. Every time we focus in on energy using a technique, the technique allows us to focus in on only a portion of the energy in the balloon instead of allowing us access to the totality of that energy. It doesn't make much difference *which* technique we use, even if the technique says we access *qi* or *ki* or *prana* or any other name implying the totality of life force. That's because *technique itself* is what limits our full access. Although technique can *grant* you introductory access, it simultaneously constricts your overall area of access. It's ironic how the same criteria that lets you in can also hold you back. We feel this constriction subconsciously, which in turn seduces us to keep learning new techniques.

Like potato chips, you can't eat just *one*. If you eat enough of them, you may reach a temporary point of not wanting to eat any more, yet you're never really satiated, satisfied or fulfilled for long because there's no real sustenance to them. So you eventually have to go hunting for another and another. And tomorrow? Who knows? Maybe another whole bag of chips. Maybe this time with sour-cream-and-chive flavoring!

Try this concept: Think of the entirety of energy as a bag of marbles (a really, really, really *big* bag), and that you can access all of it. But when you use a technique, it limits you to *accessing* just one of those marbles, to *being* just one of those marbles, rather than all the marbles. Try another technique and you get another marble, but not all the other marbles, not even the one you just got from the previous technique. Each technique allows us to pluck one marble, and only one marble. And all the other marbles, even those we had before from other techniques, fall away. As Pablo Picasso said, "The more technique you have, the less you have ... The more technique there is, the less there is." Although he was talking about the art of drawing and painting, it's equally applicable to the art of healing.

An overview of religion brings us another analogy. The world is filled with many religions, each with a window into different understandings, dimensions and perspectives into the nature of God, Love and the Intelligence of the Universe.

Many people grow up their entire lives looking out at the world through just one of these windows, possibly the same window that their parents, grandparents and great-grandparents looked out of. Many hope that their children and their children's children will look out through that same window. One window may view out onto a church, one onto a synagogue, one a mosque and another a temple or possibly a shrine or other place of worship. Other windows may look out onto nature, such as beaches, trees and mountains.

Many people who look out through their chosen window want, believe and/or are invested in their window being the *right* window. Because if someone *else's* window is the right window, it might mean that their own is the wrong window, and that possibility has the potential to negate the point of view of their entire family lineage. The prospect that we could be looking out the wrong window is so upsetting that we often fight, argue, even kill and murder people who have different window views.

But let's say one day fate touches in the form of a new friendship. As we become closer with this new friend, we realize they are looking out a different window. Yet something within us allows us to feel so good, comfortable and connected with this person that we decide to take a *quick* peek out their window. Just a quick one. Just maybe the *briefest* of glances we tell ourself. Yet in that moment of openness and insight, we see *something ... something* that at first appears to be a little different than what we've been used to seeing. Curiosity seeps in and we begin to entertain the *possibility*, only a possibility, mind you, that something we see through their window may be a *different aspect* of what we've been seeing our entire life through our own window. It's something new, something possibly *familiar*, like another facet. But not a contradiction.

As a result, our understanding shifts and we realize that if another person's window shows another aspect of the same picture we've been looking at, it's not necessarily conflictual or contradictory at all. Instead, it may simply be an *expansion* of our view. A further *illumination* of our perspective. Maybe there's a church *and* a synagogue, maybe there's a beach *and* a mountain. Maybe we become so intrigued that we decide to start looking out a few more windows, and then a few more, and this in turn grows and expands our perspective on God, Love and the Intelligence of the Universe.

Yet even if we look out of each and every window, it won't be enough to see the whole picture because each view is limited by the window frame, and even further limited by the wall that supports the frame. In reality, it's only when we're willing to go outside (figuratively speaking), beyond the limitations of the windows, the frames, the walls, floors and ceilings, maybe even go up onto the roof, that we can suddenly see in all directions.

But what happens if we bring our window frame up to that party on the roof, if we attempt to *add* technique to what is otherwise technique-free? Does it become an addition or a reduction? Can it expand our view? Of course not. All it can do is contract our view to fit *within* the frame.

With respect to energy healing, techniques *are* window frames. With respect to a balloon of energy, techniques keep us limited to specific subsets of that energy.

In the energy healing world it's not the *specific* technique that's the limiting factor, *it's technique itself!* After all, it's technique that places the frame around our view. The limitation doesn't rest with any one window frame over another. It's the employment of a window frame, any window frame, that limits our perspective.

Because Reconnective Healing is *not* a technique, we release the construct of the frame altogether. This allows us multiple gifts on multiple levels. First, it allows us to access the *entirety* of the energy within our four-dimensional balloon. Second, *because* we can access the energy in its entirety, as our balloon over time continues to expand and become more permeable, we evolve beyond energy as we've known it to be and into the timelessness of the new light and information.

This means we're no longer limited to subsets of energy in a balloon or to an individual marble from a bag, to segments or portions of healing, life force or That Which Is. By freeing ourselves from technique, we step into:

A. The entirety of energy, which leads us into ...
B. The new aspects of light and information, bringing us into ...
C. Our timeless existence.

This may well explain how, through Reconnective Healing, revitalization tends to happen so immediately, even for people who have experienced health challenges for decades, sometimes *especially* for them. And since the healings are mediated outside of time and space, this may well account for how the healings tend to last for a lifetime, how they are neither weakened nor otherwise lessened by time, and why those healed generally don't need to come back for touch-ups, realignments or maintenance healings again and again. Really, where is the freedom inherent in healing if it fosters a relationship of dependency?

RECAP: *ITs* CHARACTERISTICS

The Reconnective Healing frequencies are fairly unmistakable because they behave in a mostly uniform manner, the effects of which can be readily observed and witnessed. So with the Reconnective Healing Experience, while in one aspect it's about your *experience* with the frequencies, in another aspect it's more about your *relationship* with them. What we mean by this is that while *IT* will manifest in its own way for your highest good, the characteristics of the interaction are consistent, highly repeatable, physical, sensorial, observable and, at the same time, unique to each individual.

If we were to boil down these characteristics to their most predictable interactions, they would be:

- We *receive* the frequencies—we don't *send* them.
- The healings generally tend to last a lifetime.
- There's *no technique required* to access them. Technique actually inhibits our ability to access them fully.
- *IT's* omniscient, *IT* knows exactly where to go, what to do and how to do it.
- *IT's* tangible and observable. You can demonstrate that *IT* exists even though you can't find *ITs* parameters. Thus aspects of *IT* are measurable, which is why *IT* is recognized by science, even without there being a beginning and end, which are characteristics defining infinity.
- The frequencies become stronger with distance.

While bringing about healings for conditions that run the gamut from physical challenges to a lack of mental or emotional clarity, from broken hearts to broken bones and all the way to the level of reconnecting and restructuring *our* DNA, the DNA of *future generations* and *the evolution of humanity, IT* establishes coherence and raises the light emission in every atom of your body. *IT* does not require your direction or guidance. Instead, *IT* knows exactly what needs to be done to bring you into immeasurably greater balance on all levels: mentally, physically, emotionally, spiritually, evolutionarily and beyond. And because of its comprehensive nature as totality and oneness, *IT* encompasses, transcends and brings you the gifts of all known forms of energy healing modalities.

Because of the personal nature in which these frequencies interact, depending upon whom you ask, you will get fascinating, compelling, intriguing and *uniquely different* answers as to how these frequencies benefit them. As well, you will discover that mental, physical, emotional and spiritual healing is not so easily described as those four words might have us think. They roll off our tongues, often without much thought, yet they each contain amazing depth, levels, layers and intricacies that we tend to overlook. In the almost trite-sounding, repetitive and rote recital of these words, we often allow ourselves to become desensitized to the profound nature of what they communicate. Giving some introspection to them can enhance what we allow ourselves and, therefore, others, to receive.

On the mental and emotional level you will likely soon realize *IT* has given you increased serenity, harmony, peace and a deeper understanding of how you interact with others. This tends to transform the most difficult relationships while allowing for the emergence of more deeply fulfilling ones, whether they are old, new or renewed. Others report that their physical body's interaction with *IT* resulted in improved stamina, energy, endurance and corrected physical challenges and disabilities they had, even from birth.

On the spiritual level you will, in all probability, discover a new recognition of knowingness and a deeply profound certainty that we are in a continuous process of cocreating, facilitating and evolving into a greater expression of grace, joy and love.

As a result of your interacting with *IT*, you unearth and directly experience a new understanding of your multidimensionality. Once you learn how to recognize the frequencies, your awareness allows *IT* to be *always* available, reachable *everywhere*, in an experience of *unconditional* love.

The penultimate benefit of working with, receiving and entraining with *IT* is the revealing of our highest expression of ourselves, both as individuals and as the collective of humanity. Like an infinite *matryoshka* doll (Russian nesting doll), there are an indeterminate number of layers of understanding you uncover about yourself the more you immerse in this wordless language, including opening a new enthusiasm for your purpose in the world.

Another exquisite benefit is that it offers you an opportunity to be of service by bringing yourself and another person into greater degrees of our expansive *new known*. In the process, you heal yourself. And as you heal yourself, you heal the world.

Here's a review of some of the points in this chapter. It at first may appear to be a brief list, but as you allow yourself to really explore it, you'll find it to be quite in-depth.

We talked about the Before-Beyond, functioning outside the realms of ego, acknowledged existence not fully measurable by science, the search for parameters in that which is without parameters, awareness, simplicity, languageless language, dimensions beyond dimensions and, ultimately, being aware that we are awareness. We observed that our true nature resides outside of space and time and discovered interconnectedness through the experience of consciousness. We explored time balloons and nonlinear gifts of receiving instead of sending. Now let's play with something that we will move further into in the next chapter ... a portal into a reciprocal universe!

Exercise 2:
Active Listening/Active Awareness: An Exploration

Imperative to Reconnective Healing is active awareness.

First, let's address an obvious question: What's the difference between active awareness and passive awareness? One difference is that passive awareness tends to not require much focused awareness. For example, if a glass falls off a shelf in your kitchen, you probably don't have to be paying much attention to notice the sound it will make when it crashes on the floor. The sound will bring itself clearly to your attention.

Now let's raise the bar a bit and bring you into *active* awareness. We'll do this through an example of active listening. For this exercise, find a comfortable space that has little or no distractions. You may choose to close your eyes during parts of this exercise, so obviously don't try this while you're driving, operating heavy machinery or doing anything else that requires your eyes to be open or your undivided attention. To begin, sit comfortably somewhere and close your eyes for approximately 15–20 seconds.

Now, allow yourself to notice what ambient sounds may be present. At first you may notice the sounds of children playing outside or a car passing by, possibly the sound of birds. Next, allow your awareness to pick up on some of the more subtle sounds in the room you're in or emanating from another room, such as the sound produced by your refrigerator or another appliance, that humming sound you've become so accustomed to that you no longer recognize it's even there.

Good. Now open your eyes, relax and allow yourself to recall the sounds you just observed. By doing this, you are starting to step into a space of more active listening, a space of more active awareness.

Next, close your eyes again and listen to those sounds once more. This time, listen for varying textures, dimensions and layers of sounds occurring simultaneously. Listen for facets of a sound that are smooth and flowing and others that are more staccato. Listen for melodies and harmonies, higher and lower components, overlapping qualities and characteristics.

As you allowed yourself to explore those sounds in greater detail, you may have noticed that your body automatically began to adjust its position in relation to the sound. Your eyes may have drifted off to the left, right, up or down. This is you accessing different parts of your brain. This gives you access to different parts of your awareness. As you do this, you increase your active awareness and active listening.

Let's try it once again. But this time, after you close your eyes, *intentionally tilt your head slightly* again to one side or the other. With awareness, allow your eyes to angle up or down and off to the right or left. With awareness, allow yourself for the next 15–20 seconds to explore those sounds in even greater detail. Listen for character and quality, and take your time to observe textures, pitches and layers of sound. You will most likely observe that you are able to take in and become aware of even more aspects, details and intricacies of the sounds than you were previously noticing. Congratulations! *You're raising your active awareness level.*

At first this exercise may seem to be about *listening,* but it's about much more than that. It's about *feeling, awareness* and *receiving,* the sum of which allows you to enter into a state of *receivership.* What are you receiving? Frequencies, vibration and resonance at a more conscious level.

When interacting with the Reconnective Healing frequencies, whether as a facilitator, a client or just being open, receiving and exploring your being as awareness—in active listening—allows your being to express ITs true nature in everyday life more consistently.

1. What did I learn from this chapter?
2. What did I discover from this exercise?
3. What ideas are new to me?
4. What ideas are different than I might have thought?
5. What ideas am I now considering, contemplating?
6. Which ideas feel the most natural to me?
7. Which ideas or concepts do I have the most difficulty with or find the greatest challenge in accepting?
8. Which ideas or concepts do I have the most difficulty with or find the greatest challenge in understanding?
9. Which of my previous beliefs and ideas do I find the greatest challenge in releasing and letting go of?
10. Which ideas and concepts do I find the most freeing and empowering?
11. What has my willingness to not know already allowed me to discover? To become?
12. What might my present willingness to not know allow me to discover in the future? To become?

Please respond to the above with your thoughts, possible answers, explanations, ideas, etc., to the best of your ability.

If you don't know how to answer some of the questions above or just don't have the words, we've designed a fill-in-the-blanks model below to help you.

1. I'm not sure I know, but if I did know, the answer might be
   _____

2. I don't quite have the words to explain this, but if I did have the words, they might be _____

3. I don't quite have the words to describe this, but if I did have the words, they might be_____

CHAPTER 3

THE GIFT OF RECEIVING

"You are not a drop in the ocean. You are the entire ocean in a drop."

—Rumi

As you read this you are *receiving* at a conscious level. Although not *only* at a conscious level. At the unconscious level, you're receiving oxygen, which expands your lungs, supplies your blood and tissues and keeps you alive. At the quantum level, you're composed of endless fields of energy and receiving new aspects of light and information.

Throughout this chapter, we want you to experience a guided conversation. For a moment, picture yourself standing barefooted at the edge of the ocean looking out at the vastness of water that extends to the horizon. It is at once beautiful, expansive, majestic and inspiring. And while it is all those things, simultaneously it is also home to an entire world beneath the surface.

Now look down at your feet. Where the tides ebb and flow there exists a line that separates the ocean from terra firma. Turn around and you see the land, with its mountains, rivers, valleys, flora, fauna and lakes. It's all so beautiful. Expansive, majestic, inspiring. Zoom out farther and move up into space. Below is something even *more* beautiful, expansive, majestic, inspiring—the whole of the earth. As you look at the planet from this perspective, you can see that oceans and lands are two aspects comprising the whole. Much like the infinity symbol, the parts exist in an inherently shared interaction illustrating that you can't have receiving without giving, nor giving without receiving. This is the meaning of reception as it relates to the Reconnective Healing Experience.

More Than a Circuit

With the advent of social media causing some people to place their worth in likes and page views, it seems as if we are living in a very *me*-centric era. "Myself" is the language of separation so often misunderstood. We sometimes think that people perceive the idea of receiving as something that is selfish. In an attempt to swing the pendulum back against the tides of a *me-me-me* world, there are those who believe they need to *give-give-give* and *only* give. As receiving and giving are aspects of the same interaction, our linear language around this idea has us once again in a reverse truth.

It seems even the meaning of "receiving" has been somewhat corrupted through modern language and usage, when in actuality its etymological meaning is something quite straightforward.

In its purest essence, to receive is to *accept* into one's possession something that is offered or delivered. Another way of looking at it is to have something *bestowed* upon us—yet so many of us have confused receiving with *taking*. Here we go again. Don't believe everything you hear and think. Our use of verbal language can create confusion.

With respect to the Reconnective Healing Experience, taking is a complete misrepresentation of the interaction. In fact, the concept of receivership has nothing at all to do with taking. Instead, receiving is the defined *point of engagement* for the frequencies to be made manifest in this dimension. This occurs *through* the receiver.

The reality is, we tend to think of and understand our human lives as something that's linear, thanks in no small part to the limitation of our perceptions, senses and feelings, ultimately leading to many of our beliefs.

Accordingly, there appears to be an almost transactional element to life: the perception is that we're born, we live, we have some happy experiences, we have some not-so-happy experiences, hopefully we love and then we die. (Alright, we could have described this a bit more poetically, thrown in a few weddings and bar mitzvahs and included the part where we get to come back and do the whole thing again.)

We can take this much deeper, too. Current thinking in new quantum physics suggests we actually recycle 50 to 70 billion cells in our body every day. We move from particle to wave or, said another way, to wholeness, with the whole universe every zeptosecond (a trillionth of a billionth of a second).

All this might even eventually pose the BIG question ... On an atomic level—or any level—do we really ever die? Are we knowingly an illusion in a way? Are we the infinite modulation of Energy, Light & Information appearing real in our experience? For now, let's investigate the dual-healing experience. Particularly in the healing arts, receiving is often perceived to be linear. For example, in a healing there's a transactional exchange between the healer and the healee. The implicit dynamic is that the one being healed is in a place of lack or incompleteness, the healer has the remedy, and therefore the *understanding* is that the healer is going to *send* or *transmit* a healing to the person who lacks wholeness. *But this is an outmoded energy healing concept!*

The healing is a manifestation of infinite consciousness, the source of the universe. In this exchange, the healer and the healee become more than who they are as apparent or perceived individuals—and all the while they play the role of infinite inspiration.

Two...

that are not two...

coming together.

This is part of what may seem to be *aspects* of a circular journey that begins and ends at the same place. However, *this interaction doesn't begin and end at the same place like a simple circuit does.* Its reception is *continuous* and therefore a spiral might be a more appropriate image. As a mathematical representation of universal order, the spiral is based upon what is called the *Golden Ratio.* According to Jonathan O'Callaghan of Mailonline,"South African researchers have claimed that the universe is governed by a golden ratio. They say space-time itself is defined by [a] mathematical constant."

Spiraling Out of Control: *Thank Goodness!*
Through our understanding of the Golden Ratio, the spiral may be one of the ways we can better visualize an expanding universe, although even that is the sole experience of one reality: consciousness. Always infinite and unchanged by any experience including our own perceived expansion.

The Pyramids of Giza and Da Vinci's *Mona Lisa* were designed using the Golden Ratio. Flowers, seashells, honeybees and the human body all demonstrate the Golden Ratio. And the list goes on. However the spiral is only a good *beginning* image to gain perspective on the three-way concept of the exchange of Energy, Light & Information in the Reconnective Healing Experience, because in its design it is still linear while the healing exchange is *not*.

The place of origination and completion for the spiral is Source energy, God, Love, infinite Universal Intelligence or, as we know it to be, Energy, Light & Information. When we receive in the healing, it is not an exchange that takes place, but rather a *reorganization, a reception, a murmur...to* a *new known*.

Before we discuss the dynamics of *how*, it's important to talk about the idea of wholeness in the context of healing.

Awakening to Wholeness

Many people tend to think of the idea of healing as a return to wholeness. By that very definition, it incorrectly implies we are in a place of lack. We want to reframe this conception of healing and explain that it's not about a *journey toward* wholeness, nor is it about a *return to* wholeness—it's about our *awakening to* our ever-present wholeness. This wholeness is, has always been and will always be there. It's simply been concealed, cloaked in the circumstances of our finite existence and that can show up in the expression and activity of who we appear to be physically, mentally, spiritually and emotionally in life.

Despite the messages we are force-fed on a daily basis about how most of us are broken and in need of fixing, at the crux of Reconnective Healing is this foundational understanding: We are, always have been and always will be whole.

But in the endless societal messages about needing to fix ourselves, it can be hard to recognize the disempowering implication that we must heal ourselves and/or be healed *before* we can facilitate healing for others. This is not reception, this is a *fear-based illusion.*

If we have Parkinson's disease, a heart murmur, a limp, a cough or an ingrown toenail, should that really allow us to question whether we're fit or worthy enough to be part of the healing equation for others? *Seriously?* Do we really want the insecurity of that false belief to hold us back from sharing the gift of healing? Once we recognize that we are innately worthy and infinitely whole, any thoughts that we must first receive and demonstrate our own comprehensive wellness before facilitating healings for others, at best, is unfounded. It's time we move into the realization that a big part of our own healing comes from facilitating the healing of others. If we wait to heal ourselves, or some aspect of ourselves that we deem deficient before stepping into the role of healer, we are placing our own healing on hold and simultaneously depriving the world of a gift that each of us has to offer in the moment.

Fortunately, the Reconnective Healing Experience dismantles the perceived need for these sequential steps, conditional beliefs and rituals. This is a quantum stride forward. By removing these unnecessary enclosures that we tend to hide in, ones that erode our confidence, we step into our innate nature as healers and reclaim our wholeness in truth.

Our Wholeness Is Our Holiness

Our wholeness is that part of ourselves that remembers and knows that we exist everywhere and are interconnected to everyone and everything, *one* with everyone and everything. Our transparency is an expression of our willingness to both witness and reveal this.

That revelation (in Latin, *revelari*, meaning to lay bare, i.e., what we reclaim with the gift of direct awareness) is not something from childhood or a previous life. What we reclaim is *the pure essence of the irreducible self* that exists before-beyond without the limitation of space and time. It is the interconnectedness of formlessness experiencing the organization of our bodies as matter and form, matter and nonmatter, *IT's* holiness, *IT's* *wholeness*.

As conscious vessels, as matter with awareness connected to everything and everyone, there is no need to perceive ourselves as being separate entities just because the mental-mind and the ego create that illusion. Especially because we are in actuality integral experiences of *one* Entity.

You may find yourself asking the question, "If I'm connected to everything and a part of the whole, then who am I as an individual and what part do I play?" The part you play is EXPERIENCE! And your role as light created by light is to create and bring forth *more* light from the light. Or more poetically shared with us, "never doubt the light and love that arises *as you* every day; doubt the mental illusion that tries to convince you otherwise."
—Anonymous

Maybe our big fascination with playing our seemingly stellar individual part—rather than our roles as one with the greater whole—is what created the perception of a broken-apart *whole* to begin with.

The Reception Dynamics of the RHE

If you were to light a candle, it must first receive fire from a source. Once lit, the light from the candle casts a sphere of luminosity that radiates outwardly from the point of engagement, the wick. The wick then becomes a source of light. This is exactly what happens when we receive the Reconnective Healing frequencies. But how do we receive the frequencies? Where does this intersection appear?

To explain this, let's bring in the discoveries of Dr. Fritz-Albert Popp, a German biophysics researcher who revolutionized the study of biophotons. Biophotons are particles that exist and are stored in biological systems, and their role is to emanate and transmit light. They are mostly detectable in the ultraviolet and low-visible light spectrum. Every cell in our body produces biophotons that transmit vital communications between cells on different frequencies of light.

Picture a field of fireflies at night, then think of each firefly as a biophoton. Just as fireflies use their light for communication—to identify other members of their species or to distinguish between members of the opposite sex—biophotons also communicate data about, among other things, the state of our cells.

As a result of biophotonic communication, biophoton exchange *precedes every biochemical reaction in the body.* It's thought that the intersection of our DNA and biophoton emission is what drives the processes of the body. In Dr. Popp's words, "We know today that man is essentially a being of light. Modern science has proven it. In terms of healing, the implications of this finding are immense."

Our esteemed friend Lynne McTaggart, researcher and author of *The New York Times* best-selling book *The Field*, echoes Dr. Popp when she offers: "We are all candles. We are all emitting photons all the time." These biophotons are tiny bundles of light that exist as quantum information—living light coming from cellular DNA. Living light that must come from a source.

Our bodies are essentially composed of light, both Popp and McTaggart inform us, and the biophotons (light) that comprise our bodies are constantly exchanging information with one another. When this light is in collective coherence, McTaggart further explains, "It functions like a subatomic telephone network that operates as one giant wave or as tuning forks that resonate together. Quantum coherence means that subatomic particles are able to cooperate. They communicate like a multitude of tuning forks that all begin to resonate together ... As the waves get into *phase,* or *sync,* they begin acting like one giant wave and/or one giant subatomic particle. It's like individual instruments in an orchestra all playing in perfect orchestration."

The kind of coherence created by the biophotons serves to bring the body into tune, or optimal functioning. Different frequencies then instruct the cells to perform different functions. All of which gives credence to today's replacing of the *biochemical* model of healing with the *light* model of healing. It's this light model that could answer the question as to why instantaneous changes occur in a Reconnective Healing Experience outside of space and time.

As we know, both from the Reconnective Healing Experience itself as well as from the most prominent researchers in the field, biophotonic light clearly comes from Source itself. So when we receive, we become an inspiration for light. We also become a portal to bring more light and information into this 4D reality, both literally at the biophotonic level and figuratively as the source of inspiration for the conduit. In doing so, we become a source of light that casts a *sphere of influence.*

As we know, a sphere has no directional element, therefore the light from a candle does not go in one direction, it goes in all directions. Once your candle receives light from another source of fire, you can bring that candle into the darkness and allow those who once sat in darkness to receive the light.

Every time we allow ourselves to receive, we cast a greater light which in turn creates a greater sphere of influence to those around us. As each person's candle is lit, the collective casts a *greater* light and a *greater* sphere of influence.

This is the power of Reconnective Healing: It lights a new way toward who we truly are.

IT moves us, without any required belief in *IT,* toward the next leap in our life's journey. In doing so, *IT* shows us our expression embodied as clarity, peace, light, unity, happiness, balance, reception and love. Healing. On all levels.

When looked at through the prism of time, the whole of evolution occurs in microincrements, meaning the development of any species occurs over time through the gradual accrual of minuscule changes. The totality of changes over time adds up to the advancement of a species based on certain biological and physiological changes, making an organism better suited and more adaptable to an evolving environment. In short, every small change is part of the sum total of big change.

At some point the totality of microchanges creates critical mass, which means enough microchanges occur to produce a particular result. This is when noticeable changes occur.

From the perspective of science in the natural world, within every Reconnective Healing Experience, an expansion of direct awareness occurs. Eventually we radiate this outward and, in doing so, we can't help but cast a sphere of loving influence. Simply stated, the true nature of our being shines as the field of all experience. Or even more simply, you are essential to the greater whole.

At this moment in our experiential evolution it's important to clearly make the delineation between the concept of *receiving* versus *taking*. Receiving is a vital part of the catalytic exchange between IT and your separate self. As the receiver, you're the source for IT's experiential inspiration. Your life recognition is not only a steward to Source, but to your fellow human beings. What greater purpose could any of us hope to have in a lifetime?

Serving as the Experience of *INFINITY*

As long as our hearts are beating, we are all *reception*. This allows us to *be the* essential life force that courses through the material and matter of our bodies and through all living material and matter. When our awareness is on receiving this essence or life source and becoming its optimal inspirational expression rather than on being separate and distinct, we express and project a much more peaceful, equanimous world.

To look within is to realize that we are, each and every one of us, of Source. Yet so many look outward in their quest to understand. As more of us begin to rely on our *inner-net* rather than the *Internet*—as we further tap into this inner knowing and recognize our timeless multidimensionality—the more the Reconnective Healing Experience can swiftly usher in the next frontier of human expression, where our experience of the individual self and the universal self are the same.

The Researchers

"The highest form of ignorance
is when you reject something you don't know anything about."

—Wayne Dyer

By the time more science came to study Reconnective Healing, we already knew a few things about it. For example, the healing results have a penchant to make themselves clearly known fairly instantaneously and they tend to be lifelong. Also, the healing results oftentimes manifest before the actual scheduled, or *intended*, Reconnective Healing sessions begin.

Additionally, we knew that the energy and sensations the attendees felt in the rooms at the teaching programs and workshops' was very strong, tangible and immediate.

Reference was made to this in *The Reconnection: Heal Others, Heal Yourself,* so allow us to update you on some of the scientific data we didn't have at that time. According to pioneering quantum physicist Dr. William Tiller, Professor Emeritus from Stanford University, there's something science refers to as "positive space/time" and something else called "negative space/time."

Positive space/time is the realm of physical matter and the physical world where electricity is the primary force in electromagnetic fields. In this realm, there is a tendency toward increasing positive entropy (disorder), velocities are limited to the speed of light and likes repel and opposites attract. In this realm, energy and matter vibrate and move at speeds less than or close to the speed of light and have a basic nature that is "electromagnetic."

Negative space/time is the realm of subtle substance/spirit and the metaphysical world. This is a realm where magnetism is the primary force in magnetoelectric fields. In negative space/time there's a tendency toward increasing syntropy, order or negative entropy during which velocities are in excess of the speed of light and likes attract and opposites repel. In negative space/time, energy and matter vibrate at speeds faster than the speed of light, are magnetic in quality and have a basic nature that is "magnetoelectric." In defining this model, Dr. Tiller paved the way for new theories that explore the concept of consciousness. As a well-respected scientist, he has been central in bridging our understanding of spirituality and science.

Dr. Tiller has long had an interest in subtle energies. Perceptive people have seen, felt and reported these subtle energies for thousands of years, yet often their measurement has remained outside the limitations of many of the accepted scientific tools of the times. For that reason, they didn't always register when using standard measuring devices, yet these energies have been definitively shown to exist in more and more cutting-edge randomized, controlled and double-blind studies. Dr. Tiller became intrigued by the large body of data on these subtle energies, investing his time and applying his considerable skill to creating even more reliable equipment to detect and measure them.

By the time we met Dr. Tiller, he and fellow researcher Walter Dibble had already conducted a series of successful experiments on energy healing modalities using his most recent device. Having heard so much about Reconnective Healing, they realized that our training events would provide an ideal opportunity to continue their research. Dr. Tiller went into this research quite confident he would get the same results he had seen in his previous experiments with energy healing techniques, so he sent Dibble to conduct the initial study. Tiller and Dibble were more than surprised by the results that were unlike *any* measurements they had recorded before. So, wanting to make sure all procedures, protocols and instruments were being utilized in a uniform manner, Tiller made the unusual decision to personally supervise each subsequent phase of the study.

After conducting multiple experiments over the course of several months, he then brought in additional researchers from around the world to multiple locations where we held sessions, beginning in Sedona, Arizona, and culminating in Los Angeles, California, with numerous cities in between.

He insisted on studies at multiple locations, each utilizing the attention of diverse world-renowned researchers, because something never-before-seen was happening and the scientific world would want evidence to explain what, why and how.

The researchers took baseline readings at each venue. During this phase, they made notes on atmospheric conditions including air and water temperature, along with other data points at normal everyday levels. When the actual experiments were underway, they gathered the same data points again. The differences were then recorded and analyzed in comparison to the baselines.

To detect changes in subtle energy, Dr. Tiller, his associates and teams employed his apparatuses to calculate measurements and changes in the thermodynamic free energy in the training area.

What is *thermodynamic free energy?*
Let's break that down simply. "Thermodynamic" means temperature-related. "Free" means available. And "energy" means ... well ... *energy!* Here, Dr. Tiller and his team discovered what they called *"excess* thermodynamic free energy." In other words, more—in this case, *far more*—energy than usual that is available and responds, correlates and/or corresponds to heat and temperature changes. The temperature changes then affect and reflect what the free energy does, and the free energy affects and/or reflects temperature equivalents. In physics and physical chemistry, free energy refers to the amount of internal energy of a thermodynamic system that is available to perform work. In our case, "work" refers to evolutionary healing on all levels.

A little background: The readings were so high that initially Dr. Tiller refused to share the results with us. Instead, although not at all part of his original plan, he decided more studies would be required to verify the results of the first. He brought in renowned researchers, including University of Arizona's Dr. Gary Schwartz and Dr. Konstantin Korotkov from St. Petersburg, Russia. They confirmed that something happened at that first venue that affected the behavior of the thermodynamic free energy in a completely unanticipated manner. And the same occurrences showed in the readings at each of our subsequent training locations where he and the other researchers performed their follow-up studies. For instance, results showed that every single time, *before we even began our workshops or training events*, startling increases in energy along with extraordinary changes in atmospheric pressure were already taking place at the venues. The rooms were somehow becoming what the researchers referred to as "conditioned," days, even weeks, prior to our arrival. *Did the rooms start without us?* And was discovering that the rooms were becoming conditioned even before the training programs began part of the key to explaining why the healings often happen before the Reconnective Healing sessions are scheduled to begin?

In another way of speaking, did the RH Intelligence already arrive when the universe or the field became *aware* that there was to be a training program there? Was the RH Intelligence *already* present because it functions outside of time and space? And is it therefore not limited by the human illusion of past or future, instead always existing in *"the now"? Did the conditioning happen the moment we placed our attention on it? Did it choose to make itself known only then?*

The ultimate surprise for Drs. Tiller, Schwartz and Korotkov, however, came when they noticed that although the air temperature had only changed by a few degrees, the excess change measured in thermodynamic free energy was *the equivalent of 300 degrees Celsius, or 572 degrees Fahrenheit*! This reserved, highly articulate researcher took in an uncharacteristically long, deep breath, paused in contemplation, then muttered, "That's huge." The answers Dr. Tiller found to explain this phenomenon are tantalizing. He noticed that whenever one of us took a turn to speak to the audience, or whenever the group was practicing at their tables, there was a huge decrease in the entropy of this collective energy, in other words, a huge increase in the order or organization of the energy. The energy went from randomly free-floating, or "uncoupled" as Dr. Tiller calls it, into an ordered or "coupled" state. The only thing that could cause this, he explained, was an increase in what he calls *information production*. In other words, the excess thermodynamic free energy was in communication with *something* that told it to behave in a more focused way!

Dr. Tiller understood that the particles that make up this energy had become coupled, or *entangled,* with other particles elsewhere. He explained that this *elsewhere* is called "reciprocal space," also known as the "Reciprocal Universe." What this means is that there is a "space," or "universe," that is, for all intents and purposes, superimposed exactly where we are, and that this reciprocal space seems to hold *higher, more evolved* information.

Thoroughly mystified by it all, Dr. Tiller and his colleagues confirmed Reconnective Healing is both scientifically verifiable and reproducible.

Let's slow down here to take all this in: Wherever or whenever particles in our existence become entangled or coupled with particles in reciprocal space, *an instantaneous exchange of information occurs.* As a result, our reality instantly changes, immediately entraining to match this information. When we are in communion with the Reconnective Healing frequencies our particles are coupled/entangled with a reciprocal dimension/universe where we exist in a greater space/aspect of balance, wholeness and health. This is the compelling explanation Dr. Tiller put forward for the uniquely coherent, instantaneous healings he observed that the Reconnective Healing Experience offers. When this information, which is beyond space and time, is shared with our particles in *this* space and time (or what we perceive as the here and now), our particles benefit and transform via this interaction. This is the reason these benefits and transformations take place so immediately. If this isn't the ultimate in reception, then, really, what is?!

What seems to bring about this coherent entanglement in the Reconnective Healing training programs and sessions, as well as when you're reading books or watching Internet videos and presentations on it or going through related learning experiences, is an awareness as a participant in and of this reciprocal Universe and how we focus our attention on *IT*.

As the research shows, even as you listen to our instructors and speakers, the energy becomes increasingly more focused. As you continue on your journey with Reconnective Healing, you will probably notice syntropy, order, in other aspects of your life as well as you clearly observe your life's rapidly enhancing progress. We strongly encourage you to share your observations of these dramatic changes in your life with us.

Within You, Through You, Around You

Curiosity is ingrained in our very nature. It's instinctual and at the core of human design. Across cultures, religions, sexual orientations, gender identities, creeds and races, curiosity is a universal design that's part of a much larger picture than even some of our pivotal childhood influences including our parents or schoolteachers—who might, at times, have grown weary from our constant "why, why, why"—may have contemplated.

Why? Because our human DNA reminds and *inspires* us to inquire about the nature of life and reality. This is, after all, one aspect of how the universe comes to know itself—through our self-inquiry, curiosity and, ultimately, through our *participation* in its mystery.

You see, each time we gain an insight, each time we grow in our consciousness even when it is only by a single proton within a single atom within us, it doesn't stop there. A larger awareness is brought into being because that one proton is shared with another proton, and the proton next to it and the one across the way. And in a proton in corresponding tissue or in another part of the body. And in a proton in the person next to you and a proton in someone across the room, across the hall, across the state and in a person you may be thinking about in a different part of the world. It will even be shared with a person you're *not* thinking about, a person you haven't met and a person you might soon meet. And it will then likely be shared with a proton in an apple tree, hence becoming part of an apple to be eaten by someone in the future. Most fascinatingly, it will ultimately affect *every proton in the universe.* As Nassim Haramein, Director of The Resonance Project Foundation, posits, "In Unified Field Quantum Physics, it is generally assumed that one proton contains all the information of all other protons. In every one of your protons lies the answers to what's going on anywhere in the universe."

We could say, then, that every time you experience or learn something, you are modifying the very structure of space-time through the expansion of your consciousness. You see, the growth and expansion of the universe is dependent upon your own continued growth, evolution and expansion—and this is dependent upon your unbridled innate curiosity. Ultimately, in our curiosity and recognition that space-time is limited to our localized experiences and perceived lifetimes, we finally release the attachment and limitation imposed by the space-time construct. This allows us to receive the gift of all healing in the infinite awareness of ONE unlimited consciousness expressed in the Reconnective Healing Experience.

The Reconnective Healing frequencies
expand even what we've known as The Field
as they introduce new aspects of Energy, Light & Information—
the infinite murmur of the infinite—
in you,
around you...
always with you—
solely and soul-ly.
There are times when you allow yourself to see this,
times when you may not,
and times when you may see once again.
But know that *IT* doesn't come and go...
you do!

IT is always here.

IT is constant—

it is the *experience* of *"myself"* that is inconstant, discontinuous.

if *IT* appears to *not* be present,

it is *myself* who has turned away.

the frequencies are ever-present—

I need only rest,

rest in the knowing,

the knowing of I AM

Being.

Language and ideas have the power to transform us, but nonverbal communications can also transform us at the level of our essence. After all, does the drop of water *know* it contains the entirety of the ocean? Does it *need* to know it's composed of two hydrogen atoms and one oxygen atom for it to exist in its true nature?

The most beautiful thing is that you don't need to understand how this sphere of loving influence works, you need only be the experience of it.

Giving and receiving are part of the same energy; inhale/exhale, up/down, north/south. They are all parts of the same whole. This is something that's all too frequently overlooked when we hear the verse, "It's better to give than to receive." It's easy to miss the deeper meaning that to truly give, we *must* receive.

Ultimately, the gift of receivership allows us to transform, and in our self-transformation we enable the transformation of everything and everyone to at once become the receiver and the signal. A living Bluetooth, transforming the Universe!

Some people believe their connectedness to Source should be *solely* served through the lens and perspective of religion or nature or other specific aspects of our humanity. The Reconnective Healing Experience *removes* our finite lenses and the limitations of beliefs. *IT* is about connectedness, receiving and participating in the mystery. In awareness of who we are, the mystery discloses itself.

A notable example of an active participant in the mystery is the nineteenth-century Londoner, Michael Faraday, who had no formal education but possessed an insatiable curiosity. Faraday, along with James Clerk Maxwell, a wealthy Scottish aristocrat, redefined modern physics by describing how electromagnetic forces work. This understanding gave birth to modern communications.

With the introduction of a new concept called the "field," Faraday and Maxwell—arguably science's greatest odd couple—together upended what had been accepted (and mostly unchallenged) for more than two centuries: Newtonian physics.

What made this "electrodynamic duo" so powerful was that Faraday could see physics with his mind's eye and Maxwell could provide the undergirding mathematical support. Their discovery suggested an entirely new understanding of the structure of the universe. The world was no longer only made up of particles floating freely in space, but rather particles connected through a field. In Faraday's words, "No matter what you look at, if you look at it closely enough, you are involved in the entire universe." His point being there's a greater mystery that exists, a reality in which we don't need to believe or even understand, one we need only to participate in. Or, in Albert Einstein's wisdom, "There comes a time when the mind takes a higher plane of knowledge but can never prove how it got there."

Which brings us to the beauty of the Reconnective Healing model. It's simple, and yet the outcome is revolutionary. It opens a healing bandwidth accessible to all of us that transcends the perceived limitations of today's science and its capacity to explain it.

At some future time, however, the next Maxwell may show up to demonstrate the existence in mathematical terms. Fortunately, we don't need to put our lives or our healing on hold in anticipation of that. Today's research on Reconnective Healing isn't designed to prove whether or not it exists, science acknowledged its existence a long time ago. They're only trying to figure out *how* it does what it does. And that understanding is, at best, a long way off, if at all.

By learning to recognize and receive *IT*, without preconceived agendas or any form of preparation, we are able to instantaneously establish and integrate a more coherent level of balance in all aspects of life experience. Reception is learning to receive *us*, learning to receive *being*, learning to receive our *essence*, without question, without doubt, hesitation, ambivalence, illusion or judgment.

The Reconnective Healing Experience transforms our bodies, hearts, minds and overall life progress in ways that otherwise might seem implausible. Being able to direct our attention without intention, expectation, judgment or even belief is part of the expanded gifts and freedom of infinite intelligence.

Here's a review of some of the points we covered in this chapter:

We've now explored our beginningless/endless/infinite existence as circuitry, an awakening to ever-present wholeness, that we are made of "star stuff," that we exist as holiness in our "wholiness," our role as receivership and that we are human candles producing, emitting and exchanging biophotons of light. We discovered excess free thermodynamic energy that appears in anticipation of us as well as Energy, Light & Information that is seeking us. And we learned to open a portal to the reciprocal universe through the simplicity of reception. So let's explore our existence as circuitry in this exercise.

Exercise 3:
A Circuit Party Worth Raving About

Let's begin by taking a moment to explore what we'll call "normal anatomic position" of the hand. This is medical terminology for the position your hands automatically assume when you're not conscious of them. To find your normal anatomic position, simply allow your arms to fall to your sides, allowing your hands to hang loosely. Gently shake them a little to release any residual tension. Without moving them, look down and notice the position they've fallen in to: fingers gently curved, most likely not touching one another. This is their normal anatomic position. It's the position, give or take, that you'll want your hands to remain in while you play and explore. This is a position of ease. If we want to assist people with, among other issues, "dis-ease," then we want to begin from a position of "ease" ourselves. This concept of ease permeates every aspect of Reconnective Healing. Our hands are held in a position of ease, we keep our bodies in a place of ease, our minds and thought processes remain in a state of ease and, as much as possible, if you are working with a client, you'd like the client to be at ease also.

These frequencies are highly and unmistakably palpable. The exact sensations you experience may differ from moment to moment and even from one hand to the other, yet will most likely become incontrovertibly present. It's common to experience everything from tingling, throbbing, cold, heat, pushing and pulling, to a feeling of a breeze or wind coming through your hands. And if you're not sure you're noticing palpable sensations, relax and receive. They'll show up at the appropriate moment. Probably when you least expect them.

This variability of this experience is important to remember because we tend to throw judgment onto many things we experience, notice or don't think we notice, based on the stories we've heard. For example, we often think of a healer's hands as being warm, considering cold to not be indicative of healing but rather indicative of sickness or death. In many Asian schools of healing, heat represents healing from the earth and cold represents healing from the heavens. Neither is better or worse than the other. It's time we let go of some of these limiting and defining boxes and allow ourselves to enjoy an expanded perspective on the larger picture. It's this variability, and the infinite flow, that allows for what's most appropriate to come through. This process is self-regulating, self-determining, self-adjusting and always perfectly responsive.

Reconnective Healing provides a perspective on these beliefs that points out the futility of trying to attribute specific meaning to them. The sensations that come to you are specifically a part of *your* process, representative of what *you* need and are receiving.

OK. So that's fine. But what does it *mean* when you feel, actually *feel,* these unexpected sensations in your hands? It's as if you were given certain kinds of latent receptor cells with appropriate DNA encodements designed to "switch on" and bring you into a more cognizant awareness and receptivity as these frequencies become more available. And now is that time. The receptivity is there; it's an element of who you are from this point forward.

Responding to the Energy

Another thing about the sensations you're probably starting to feel is that they vary in intensity as well as character and will tend to make themselves unmistakably known. If you previously studied any energy healing techniques, you will discover that you may no longer distinctly feel those energies. It's not that those energies are "lost." They're still here. It's more as if they were washed over by and incorporated into the Reconnective Healing frequencies, much as an ocean wave washes over and incorporates into it a tiny puddle on the shore. Although we may never find that specific puddle again, it isn't lost; it's simply become part of a greater whole. In other words, *you've* begun to ascend into the greater whole.

So, for this exercise, bring your hands into the normal anatomic position you just discovered, starting with your hands approximately a foot apart from each other, palm facing palm. Now, bring the ring finger of your right hand down a little bit until it appears to be pointing into your left palm. Place your attention and awareness in your left palm and, with a slow, small, continuous circular movement of that ring finger, even though it's still approximately a foot away from your other hand, imagine it drawing a continuous circle onto your left palm. Notice what you feel. Are you able to feel that circle being drawn by your right ring finger?

Now let's play a little. Slowly pull your left palm further and further away to your left. Then slowly pull your right hand further to your right. Notice how you can still feel that sensation. When your hands are two or three feet apart, hold them still and reverse the direction your ring finger is circling in. And notice how fairly immediately the sensation in your left palm reverses itself to correspond to the new direction your right ring finger is moving in. Play with the speed of movement of your ring finger. Notice, too, how the speed of movement of your ring finger affects the speed of movement of the sensation in your left palm. It doesn't have to be your ring finger. We're using it for this exercise because it's movement tends to be the lightest, gentlest and often the least distracting finger to work with in this manner.

Now, let's step into something a little more subtle. While holding your hands still and maintaining a distance of one–three feet between them, let go of the circular movement of your ring finger and, instead, make the tiniest, subtlest vertical and/or horizontal movements with it. Maybe starting with movements that are only an inch up and down or sideways, then a half-inch, then a quarter-inch or even less.

OK. That's fairly simple, right? Now let's explore subtlety into a greater infinite ... Again, while holding your hands still and maintaining that one–three-foot distance, also hold your ring finger still. And *imagine* it continuing those tiny vertical and/or horizontal movements. Notice what you feel in your left palm. Now imagine the circular movements. Imagine them larger, then smaller. Faster, then slower. Then move your ring finger in the pattern you were imagining. Then go back to simply imagining. Take your time with each of these. Observe how the intensity of sensation varies with and without movement. Play with the interaction both with the physical movement and without.

The question becomes, is it imagination or observational awareness? Then the question becomes how can you distinguish between the two? And then the question becomes ... is there a distinction? And then more questions come.

What if imagination were a tool to discover truth? An invisible net? A magnet? A dream catcher of sorts? When a bone breaks in half, on an X-ray there clearly appears to be nothing between the two pieces of broken bone. Yet gradually, over time, through viewing a series of X-rays of the same fracture, you can begin to see the space between the two pieces of bone becoming a milky white. The milky-white area becomes a denser and denser white, eventually becoming fairly opaque. And one day, weeks to months later, the two pieces of bone become one again. In other words, that empty space between them becomes solid bone again. How does that happen? Because the space was never *empty* in the first place. It was a field, invisible to the naked eye, that slowly attracted particles of calcium, magnesium and phosphorus. As enough of those particles became attracted to this field, the bone became more and more visible and solid. One might say it became more and more *real*.

The funny thing is, *it was always real.* And just as the space between broken pieces of bone is never really empty, imagination is never a formed concept of something "not actually present," of emptiness. Imagination is a key that opens a door to greater recognition of your observational awareness and to as-of-yet undiscovered experiences. Throughout this book, that's exactly what we are about to discover, a greatly expanded awareness, one that comprises us and the entire universe.

So, are you feeling energized, stimulated, motivated or just plain *you-know-what* curious? Then let's play one more time. Here we go:

Hold your hands still.

Move the ring finger of one hand in tiny little circles while you allow yourself to feel it in your opposite palm.

Now move it in your mind only and feel it in your opposite palm.

Breathe in...

Feeling inspired?

Good!

Now exhale.

Pause...

Gently inspire another breath...

Play with exploringly small and slow movements again.

This time notice how the feeling in the still hand expands.

Observe how the feeling in the moving hand also expands.

Where else in the head or body do you feel it?

Does the sensation stay the same? Or does it change or vary?

Does it occupy the same space? Or does it expand?

What other characteristics of sensation and observational awareness do you recognize?

Let your eyes gently drift off, maybe to the left or to the right, and look within *you* for greater awareness of the sensations as they make themselves and their presence more recognizable.

Now hold your gently moving hand still and slowly move the other.

Now hold both hands still, gently moving one in your mind, then the other.

Explore, play and discover the intricacies and intimacies of our interconnectedness with ourselves and with the universe.

1. What did I learn from this chapter?
2. What did I discover from this exercise?
3. What ideas are new to me?
4. What ideas are different than I might have thought?

5. What ideas am I now considering, contemplating?

6. Which ideas feel the most natural to me?

7. Which ideas or concepts do I have the most difficulty with or find the greatest challenge in accepting?

8. Which ideas or concepts do I have the most difficulty with or find the greatest challenge in understanding?

9. Which of my previous beliefs and ideas do I find the greatest challenge in releasing and letting go of?

10. Which ideas and concepts do I find the most freeing and empowering?

11. What has my willingness to not know already allowed me to discover? To become?

12. What might my present willingness to not know allow me to discover in the future? To become?

Please respond to the above with your thoughts, possible answers, explanations, ideas, etc., to the best of your ability.

If you don't know how to answer some of the questions above or just don't have the words, we've designed a fill-in-the-blanks model below to help you.

1. I'm not sure I know, but if I did know, the answer might be _____

2. I don't quite have the words to explain this, but if I did have the words, they might be _____

3. I don't quite have the words to describe this, but if I did have the words, they might be_____

CHAPTER 4

THE GIFT OF MINDFUL MINDLESSNESS

*"It is a thorny undertaking, and more so than it seems, to
follow a movement so wandering as that of our minds, to
penetrate the opaque depths of its innermost fields, to pick
out the innumerable flutterings that agitate it."*

—*Michel de Montaigne*

*"I put my heart and my soul into my work,
and have lost my mind in the process."*

—*Vincent Van Gogh*

There are many wonderful self-help books and techniques available to help us
manage our thinking—our thinking and doing, doing and thinking, even our
thinking about doing and thinking! At the same time, we know that we're not
only more than our thoughts and our physical bodies, but that we also *exist* in
an organization beyond what our minds and thoughts can perceive.

More accurately, it's *prior* to thought, *prior* to mind, *prior* to time.

Welcome to *Mindful Mindlessness* in the Before-Beyond.

Losing your mind to Energy, Light & Information is akin to no longer
having to worry about putting your foot to the pedal when driving your car.
It's as if your hands are on the steering wheel, your eyes are on the road and
you're simply moving along. There isn't acceleration or deceleration for you to
concern yourself with. It's steady, graceful, continuous, smooth and timeless.
This momentum can produce a whole new level of clarity and quality of life.

Speaking of losing your mind, can you remember the first time *you* lost yours? Or the first time you *allowed* yourself to *let go* of yours? Even for a moment? We've all likely experienced this feeling once or twice in our lifetime. *Reader advisory: We're not talking about a psychotic break here, but rather* exquisitely *losing your mind!*

So, how do we allow ourselves to lose our mind to Energy, Light & Information? The answer is you and your attention simply *dissolve* into *IT.* And, in doing so, *IT* captures your attention. IT maintains you with your awareness and attention in perfect balance. You're not dwelling on the past or anticipating your future—you're observing and feeling without judgment or attachment to any thoughts.

Could this experience of awareness and nonattachment be what philosophers, mystics and saints have been talking about as the eternal present moment? Is this what St. Francis of Assisi meant when he said, "Wear the world as a loose garment?"

Dr. Rollin McCraty of HeartMath Institute calls this a state of *quiescence.* In *The Coherent Heart: Heart–Brain Interactions, Psychophysiological Coherence, and the Emergence of System-Wide Order,* Dr. McCraty and his colleagues describe quiescence as "the intrusion of mental and emotional 'chatter' is reduced to a point of internal quietness, to be replaced by a profound feeling of peace and serenity and a deep sense of being centered in the heart."

In this quiet stillness, a hyperawareness exists where there is no division. Previously, quiescence was something that only master meditators, Buddhist monks and others of that ilk were thought to be able to achieve, and only after years of practice. Yet those in a Reconnective Healing Experience seem to enter this quiescence the moment they become aware of this reception, consciously or unconsciously.

When researchers at the University of Arizona first started measuring heart and brain waves both of the practitioners as well as the recipients during their Reconnective Healing Experiences, they found that the participants, including those who *didn't* feel, notice or even believe in the frequencies, exhibited involuntary physical registers that were visibly observable along with involuntary registers that were observable on printouts of their heart and brain scans.

Because the Reconnective Healing frequencies do not engage with the thinking mind, this is not about the mental state of mindfulness—it's about what might be termed *Mindful Mindlessness*. The frequencies aren't interested in our thoughts or belief systems any more than the sun seeks to know how or why it shines. *IT* has no limitation or bias based upon any circumstance in our health, wealth, intelligence, personality, success, failure, gender, religion, sexual preference, skin color, hair color or whether we are accessing the latest technological gadgets. Our role is simply to receive, observe, notice, witness and be *ITs* experience.

"You need to spend your time clearing the path, clearing the path for your greater energy to come through; and it will, if you are just consciously aware of That Which Is as it is being fulfilled. And you must feel this with your life." To understand this quote from Eric and Frederick Ponzlov's book *Solomon Speaks on Reconnecting Your Life*, you want to understand that *That Which Is* being fulfilled is different than you feeling fulfilled by *That Which Is*.

The point of engagement with the frequencies exists somewhere *prior* to our thoughts, *prior* to our thinking mind, in the before-beyond and in the background of all known experience. The moment we start intending, directing, controlling, expecting or predicting outcomes in our exchange with *IT*, our receptivity to infinite potential diminishes and becomes obscured with increasing opacity. Despite the intentions of our mind and the needs of our personality to impose order and control over everything, *IT* patiently waits for us to return. In *Oneness*, the knowingness that you are enough becomes your *new known*.

> *"There comes a time when the mind takes a higher plane*
> *of knowledge but can never prove how it got there."*
>
> —*Albert Einstein*

Diving Deeper into Knowingness

Knowledge is a collection of steps that lead us to a jumping-off point where we may enter into knowingness: a fieldless, stateless, pure consciousness/awareness. In today's complex world, moving beyond our thoughts is an acquired and necessary artform because the way we're constantly bombarded with information doesn't allow us to live our best and most joyful existence otherwise. If we're not paying attention and being aware of our awareness, our presence and our being, well, it's easy for the mind to get swept away into a deluge of data that brings no real value or meaning to our lives.

When we get out of the cerebral mind, we move into love and connectedness. The thinking mind is constantly creating a narrative that attempts to help us make sense of ourselves. In creating that narrative, however, we can't help but compare ourselves to others, driving our separate-self deeper into the ego's story of all things separate and distinct. Another way we can visualize this is that these narratives lead us into enclosures within our finite reality. These enclosures tend to ignite a pattern where people place themselves in a constant state of comparison and, as a result, believe there is something wrong with them. This has inspired a market for self-help books proclaiming that all you need to do is change these five things about yourself and you'll be happy, change these three things about yourself and you'll find joy, change this one thing and you'll find love. The discernible subtext here: *Nothing about you is OK the way you are.* This is *definitely* not a recipe for healing.

Fortunately, the Reconnective Healing experience interrupts this cognitive messaging through a nonverbal, tangible and kinesthetic interchange whereby you are propelled into a self-recognizable and autoreinforcing state of worthiness. Self-sabotaging programs seem to vanish for good. It's an interchange where *your healing becomes the awareness of your wholeness.* The Intelligence reaches to you and the frequencies engage you, entrain with you and bring about the most appropriate healing for you in wholeness.

Instinct vs Intuition

"Instinct is something which transcends knowledge. We have, undoubtedly, certain finer fibers that enable us to perceive truths when logical deduction, or any other willful effort of the brain, is futile."

—*Nicola Tesla*

How do birds know when it's time to fly south for the winter and north for the summer? Do they get together at the Toucan Lounge for Happy Hour on

Thursdays after Bird Bingo and vote on the best time to fly? It's not through knowledge that they migrate—it's through an innate, inner knowing, a shared state of knowingness accessed and attained through frequency and vibration.

Researchers would say it's via information from the sun, the stars and by sensing the earth's magnetic field. Science would refer to this as coherence. As birds tap into this knowingness, into the essence and nature of their true being, they become part of a much larger ecosystem and tapestry of existence. In doing so, their travels allow them to better contribute to the health of the planet through pollination, seed dispersal and, in essence, through simply *being* birds. Rather than just being birds who inhabit *birdness*, they become an aspect of a much larger beneficial consequence of the ecosystems they inhabit, and the entire planet as a whole.

If birds instinctively know how to behave, maybe we do too! So that just as birds know when to migrate, something inherent drives the desires of every living organism, including humans.

Unlike birds, however, we are quite possibly the only (or one of the only) animals that attempts to outthink our gut or otherwise override our inner knowingness through thought and reason. We ignore our instinct and instead replace it with what we call our *intuition*. When talking about instinct versus intuition, we find that people often blur the lines, but there is a clear delineation between the two.

Instinct is not merely a *feeling*. A familiar and surface-level definition is that it's an innate, inborn pattern of activity. Derived from the Latin word *instinctus* (meaning impulse), it's considered a "hardwired" tendency toward a particular common behavior that occurs within biological species. On a deeper and more comprehensive level, however, instinct is an *instantaneous knowingness*—so instantaneous, in fact, that apparently it bypasses the endless strings of bioelectrical signals that create thought. Your instinct is your *instantaneous and unquestioning knowingness*. It is unfettered, unobscured, unconfused and uncluttered by thought and opinion because instinct is *prior* to thought. *Prior to thought.*

Intuition comes from the Latin word *intuitio*, meaning "a looking at or consideration." It's a process whereby information too complex for rational thinking alone is sorted through. This process is learned, not innate, and based on an accumulation of beliefs and experiences up to that point in a person's life that are then brought into their decision-making process.

So, on one hand, you have instinct, an innate and instantaneous certainty and knowing, and on the other you have intuition, which is learned and, to varying degrees, permeated with and clouded by thought and opinion. It brings to mind "a gilding of the lily"—an idiom derived from an often-misquoted passage of Shakespeare's that describes the process of adorning something that's already beautiful.

> *Therefore, to be possess'd with double pomp,*
> *To guard a title that was rich before,*
> *To gild refined gold, to paint the lily,*
> *To throw a perfume on the violet,*
> *To smooth the ice, or add another hue*
> *Unto the rainbow, or with taper-light*
> *To seek the beauteous eye of heaven to garnish,*
> *Is wasteful and ridiculous excess.*
> —*The Life and Death of King John* by Shakespeare, 1595

Intuition uses the mind, layering or gilding a level of thought on top of our instinct, the lily, adding a filter that dilutes instinct's purest form. The mind and the thoughts it produces, along with critical thinking, may well be significant contributors to what's brought us to this point in our evolution. Simultaneously, they may well be holding us back from the next phase of our evolution.

In ancient Greece, where this type of Western thinking originated, the Greeks called it *philosophia* (philosophy), which means *the love of wisdom*. The esoteric understanding of wisdom, however, comes from nature. It's not something that comes from our thinking mind, rather, it comes from *beneath our conscious awareness*, the place of our spiritual thinking.

Visionary theoretical physicist Stephen Hawking once hypothesized that for us to actually become a multidimensional human form, we need to move beyond thought alone, our technological advancement does not guarantee the future of civilization or spiritual evolution. This may be an excellent moment to consider growth, not so much as an expansion of things in matter and structure, but rather growth in what matters most—oneness and unity. Because humanity has been focused for so long on growth and progress as analytical and cognitive modalities, it's perhaps time to embrace another realm where information flows in and out without cognition in a state of *Mindful Mindlessness.*

Reception

There is the mind, and then there is the brain. Like a radio picking up signals, the brain (although not the brain exclusively) is the receiver that absorbs energy and light from the field in the form of frequencies and vibrations, which it then transduces into information. Much like a radio, we could say the brain is the receptive component. The mind, however, is where the information is analyzed to make determinations. It's where reason, thought and evaluation occur.

When we experience Reconnective Healing in Mindful Mindlessness, the brain is receiving. It is designed for the infinite reception of Energy, Light & Information. Again, it's important to draw a distinction between the brain and the mind. In the healing experience, our job is not to contemplate or reduce this reception to information our mind can understand through analysis. Once we begin to analyze, we're no longer receiving, we're directing. Our role is to observe, notice and experience. We have a choice: to *be* in it, *merge* with it and *become* it—or remain *outside* of it, *contemplate* it, *evaluate* it and therefore *judge* it.

If you wanted to know the ocean, would you be satisfied to merely sit on the shore and contemplate it? Wouldn't you really prefer to jump into the fullness of its experience?

Bottom line: We don't need to introduce a thought process into Reconnective Healing because it doesn't operate at the level of our thoughts. It operates prior to thought, prior to us reducing it through thought. We are simply and fantastically the catalyst. *IT* reaches *to* us and moves *through* us to *establish* us as the receiver signal. Our purpose is to be consciously aware of That Which Is, as it is being fulfilled. And then feel this with our life.

At this intersection, we are the catalyst and, as such, able to facilitate healing, able to *be* the healer as well as to *become the healing itself.*

As the witness and the witnessed, we can observe changes in another's healing equation without the need for cognitive evaluation. So in a Reconnective Healing Experience, although you're witnessing loving Intelligence orchestrate a seamless melding and a profound transformation of the physical, mental, emotional and spiritual —and you are witnessing it occur within, for and about the person you're in reception with—you're not required to be cognitively involved in the process. In fact, it's best that you aren't: that's better for them and better for you. There's no need for opinions or interpretations of what's occurring. You're simply the witness and the witnessed. And, in your perfection, exquisitely so!

The Lady in the Garden: A First-Hand Account

At age 11, I awoke one morning in a panic. I was so hot that I couldn't breathe well. As I reached up to wipe the sweat from my face, I realized that not only were my hands swollen to twice their size, my face and tongue were, also. I could hardly see my mother standing in front of me, for my eyes were almost swollen shut. She was trying to get me to take some medicine. Although this was not the first of these incidents, this was the worst. My mom put me in the car and took me to the emergency room. I was so scared, I thought for sure I was going to die. Mom kept saying, "Don't worry, honey, it's going to be all right. We're all here to take care of you." She's a registered nurse; it's part of her job to soothe people. But it only got worse.

I spent the next couple of days in bed, and the nights with my mom in the emergency room where she worked. I had these strange blotches all over me, and some turned into big welts. All my joints were swollen, and my whole body ached. The doctors didn't know what was wrong; they had never seen a kid with so many odd things at once. So, they sent me to a specialist. Months of tests and different medications revealed that I had rheumatoid arthritis and mixed connective tissue disease. The doctor said this could include lupus, but the test was inconclusive. The course of action for this, you ask? Ten—yes, ten!—Bayer aspirin per day for six weeks, and no stressful activity, not even gym class.

Several years passed, I had learned to accept the pain—worse, to accept the "We don't know what's wrong" answer. I learned to smile and put on a good show for everyone. It's much harder than people think, and of course, the smile and good show didn't last forever. I did fairly well for several years; however, by age 20, I was worn out, depressed and forcing myself to get out of bed for work. So, once again, I saw several different doctors who now said I had severe depression. I spent the next year trying various assortments of antidepressants, which made life easier to deal with but did not make my body feel any better. Looking back, I can see why I was depressed: You would be too if you felt as bad as I did every day. I finally went to a doctor who ran a number of tests based on my childhood history and concluded that I was not simply depressed, but that my earlier diagnosis of lupus appeared to be correct. Again I was put on a varied array of medications, none of which worked for more than a few weeks.

I next went to a specialist, a rheumatologist. We tried other medications, some made me sick, some gave me hives and, eventually, some worked. Sadly for me and my mother, they didn't work well for long, and were very expensive. So, although there is no medically known cure for lupus, my mom started looking for a more permanent form of treatment.

One day while watching a high-profile television talk show, she saw a healer: Dr. Eric Scott Pearl. She made all the arrangements for me to see him before she told me anything about him. It wasn't until we were making that first six-hour trip that she told me he was an alternative healer, that he wasn't going to touch me and that I was going to feel better. I laughed at her and strongly suggested that she might be in need of some professional psychiatric counseling. She replied, "What do you have to lose?" Who could argue with that after everything I'd been through? Besides, she knew enough not to tell me until we were well underway in the car.

So, we arrived at my 11 a.m. appointment with me, thinking, "This guy must be a quack." In the healing room was a table to lie on, soft lighting and sounds playing in the background. An aide told me to take off my shoes, lie down and relax. Easy for her to say. I tried but couldn't.

Dr. Pearl came in a few minutes later, and to my surprise, he looked pretty nor- mal. We talked for a few minutes about my major complaints, which were my hands. He asked me to hold up one of them. He held his hands on either side of mine but did not touch me. He began to move his hands around in this slow, circular motion. Suddenly, I was scared because there was this breezy feeling over my hand and this overwhelming smell of flowers. Flowers like I had never smelled before. I thought, OK, this is really strange. His hands are moving much too slowly to create wind. And what about the flowers? How is he doing this? He then moved to my other hand, and that same windy feeling came. He asked me to close my eyes, and all I could think was, He's a freak, and I am obviously crazy!

I closed my eyes anyway, and as he slowly walked around my body, the windy feeling followed his hands. What happened next really startled me. My eyes flew wildly open and Dr. Pearl asked, "What's wrong?" I didn't dare say, but every time Dr. Pearl came near my ankle, it became very hot. This was weird, and I was not happy.

Throughout the rest of the session, I wasn't able to relax. When it was finally over, he asked what I had experienced. I told him about the windy feeling and the flower smell. He asked if I knew what the flower smell was, and I said "You." He told me he didn't think it was him, so I asked if I could smell him. "Yes," he laughed and indulged me. Sure enough, he didn't smell like a flower, and oddly enough, the smell was almost gone.

He took a few notes and told me to come to the front when I was ready. He left the room. I must have been in there for about 10 or 15 minutes looking around for a fan, some flower-scented incense, something—ANYTHING!—to explain the wind and the smell. I even took a large picture down off the wall (it was quite heavy) and moved the furniture around in my search (something I haven't even admitted to him yet). But I didn't find anything. Now more than ever, I wondered if I were going crazy. I left the room and spoke only the briefest words to the doctor. I was in a hurry to leave. This was the strangest thing that had ever happened to me. My mom and I drove home: I slept most of the way, and when I woke up, my hands didn't ache as much. I thought, Oh, it's just a fluke.

I went about the next week as usual and continued with my meds. The thought of my next appointment with Dr. Pearl loomed in my mind. I really didn't want to go, but the following week we packed up and once again headed to California. I was very nervous. I took off my shoes, climbed up on the table and, to my surprise, I was suddenly very relaxed. Dr. Pearl came in and we chatted for a few minutes about how I had been feeling, which was slightly better than usual. He then suggested I close my eyes and relax. He was about to begin.

I closed my eyes and suddenly felt an indescribable peace. I could feel the wind around my hand and the absolutely overwhelming smell of these flowers. Where is this coming from? I wondered to myself, and in that same instant, a woman appeared. I couldn't see her face, just her white dress and dark hair blowing in the breeze. She was offering her hand, standing in this amazing garden of flowers above me. It was as if she were saying, Take my hand and walk through this garden, only she wasn't speaking to me, at least not with words, and I couldn't open my eyes. I was no longer aware of Dr. Pearl's presence in the room—or was I somehow no longer in the room? How bizarre! I wanted to go. I reached out, felt a tug on my hand and boom!—I was up there in the flowers with her. Then, just as quickly as she came, she was gone.

My eyes flew open, and Dr. Pearl was finished. He asked if I was all right. I nodded. I didn't dare tell him what happened. I just wanted to leave. He walked out of the room, and this time I didn't look for anything. I just left. He and my mom were at the front desk talking when I came out. I don't think I said a word to either of them. I just headed for the door. Mom soon followed. We went outside and I started to cry. I couldn't tell her what happened, I couldn't tell anyone what happened. What would my mom think, much less what would other people think? We headed to the hotel where we were spending the evening. I had one last appointment the following day. I didn't say much the rest of the night.

The next morning came quickly. I went to the appointment, even though I really didn't want to. During the entire session, all I could think was: Isn't it over yet? It actually ended rather quickly. Dr. Pearl could sense that I didn't want to be there. I overheard him telling my mother, who was trying desperately to schedule me for another appointment, not to bring me back unless I asked to return. He told her that I didn't seem to want to be there and didn't seem comfortable with the visits. He was right. I met him out front, politely thanked him and we headed home. It was none too soon for me. I spent the next two days scouring every flower shop and plant store in the city where we lived. I had to find those flowers, or at least track down that smell again. It was as if finding them would let me know that I hadn't lost my sanity. But then, what would not finding them mean?

Try as I might, I did not find them. No one in the shops recognized them from the description of what they looked or smelled like. It's as if they didn't exist anywhere on Earth. It was about a week before I could begin to talk about what happened to me without crying. Having been an avowed atheist, this had shaken my belief system to the very core.

Since my three Reconnective Healing visits, I've improved 100 percent. I can do things now that I thought I would never be able to do again. I can get out of bed without any problem, a process that used to require a couple of hours. I can open jars, even some my boyfriend can't! I can work out and exercise without feeling like I'm falling apart. I can wear my jewelry because my hands and ankles no longer ache or swell. Best of all, no more prescription medications. And after my mother's research into the Reconnective Healing Experience, I feel a lot less crazy knowing I'm not the only one seeing these angels and taking trips through flower gardens in the sky! Now that I've brought myself to talk about it , I've discovered it's actually a relief. Some people look at me strangely when I tell them about this, but I can't let that stop me. People need to know that this type of thing does exist. Had my mother not taken me to Los Angeles, I don't know what condition I would be in today. And in return, I hope that my words can help someone else.

Our Essence: The Intersection of Reception, Our Body and Our Truth

In the Reconnective Healing Experience, it's important to understand that we are not attempting to heal any one particular *thing*. Perhaps someone's back hurts. Believe it or not, *it's not your job—nor your highest role or purpose—to heal that person's back pain,* much as we, they and their mother may have adopted that belief and desire for us to do so. We are not here to focus on symptoms. The back pain is a symptom of *something*—and that *something* is exactly what RH will address—independent of human intention. Although not limited to physical healing, *IT*, as an expression of balance and infinite order, may also operate in that place or space of the physical.

What *is* your essence? Some might call it the soul, but it's safe to say our essence is part of our nonphysical form. A quantum physicist may consider your essence to be one thing, a member of the clergy may consider it something else and an atheist, something entirely different. Authors Jeff Carreira and Jeff Hamilton describe it as a kind of new beginning: "By giving up any investment in the mind's power to know, we will discover the primordial innocence of our own true nature, which paradoxically opens the door to an infinite source of wisdom."

We would say that our essence is the truth of who we are. It's through this truth—our essence—that *IT* interacts, entrains with us and experiences itself. And here we encounter one of Reconnective Healing's most profound discoveries, most profound truths: We do not *send* the healing, we *receive* it ... we *become* it—and our very presence *accelerates and expands* it. Here we truly become a catalyst in the knowingness that a healing can happen anywhere we are. Thus, through our *attention,* not our *intention,* we become a timeless participant in a three-way interaction between our *local* embodiment (body), our *nonlocal* timelessness of being (essence) and the Before-Beyond.

Case in point: When students at our training programs begin to feel, pull, stretch and interact with the Reconnective Healing frequencies, we witness them experience a range of emotions that runs the gamut from fear and frustration to effortless freedom and liberation. As we guide them to the tables where they interact with each other, the power of three rises like the Phoenix.

This exalted recognition state is realized when we come together with another person in the murmur of Energy, Light & Information and become one: one with the other person and one with Universal Intelligence, the reunification of *humanity the physical with humanity the spiritual.*

For many peoples, cultures and religions, the number *three* bears great significance, as though endowed with mystical qualities. But three isn't just a number assigned to our origin stories and religions; it's also a very powerful number in science. For instance, it's the only prime number that is one less than a perfect square.

In traditions such as Taoism, Hinduism, Buddhism, Judaism and Catholicism, the number three also serves to give us insights into the three-fold nature of reality as well as our relationship to it. In *The Tibetan Book of the Dead,* the "Three Bodies of Buddhahood," correlate with body, mind and spirit. In Christianity, this idea could be overlaid onto the idea of the three aspects of the one God: the Father, Son and Holy Spirit. All of these under-standings lend credence to the model that a human being is one with God, Love, Source, That Which Is, Universal Intelligence, the Before-Beyond or any other name that makes you smile.

In *Living Buddha, Living Christ,* when the Vietnamese Buddhist monk Thich Nhat Hanh had a meeting with a Christian clergy, he stated, "I told the Priest that I felt all of us have the seed of the Holy Spirit in us, the capacity of healing, transforming and loving. When we touch that seed, we are able to touch God the Father and God the Son."

We appreciate how Hanh's perspective relates to Reconnective Healing: right there in the middle of what he referred to as God the Father and God the Son is *you, me and everyone else.* Although Reconnective Healing has noth-ing to do with any one religion, we mention this because Hanh presents the idea of the Trinity as *the process of direct knowing of the Divine*, a knowing that transcends all religious names, rituals and languages itself.

According to prehistoric paintings on cave walls found throughout France, Spain and other parts of the world, and later making themselves known throughout our origin stories, myths and religious texts, it seems even our earliest ancestors understood this threefold nature of human existence.

The inquisitive nature of humankind, as well as the questions that arise from the human mind are, in one sense, responsible for our evolutionary success.

They've prodded us to delve into our origins, our place in the world and in the universe. At the same time, this acquisition of knowledge has brought us to our current understanding of where we are today and who we are in this moment in history. But now it's time to move beyond knowledge, beyond the mind.

Humans are communicators by design and evolution, driven to interact with one another and the world around us. We are not only here to understand our present moment, but also to appreciate the larger, unseen aspects of our existence.

But what if there were a language beyond words that we could learn without needing to memorize vocabulary or learn grammar, syntax or other pragmatics? A universality of communication no longer defined by our stories? An all-inclusive language without any distinction related to health, wealth, gender, religious belief, cultural orientation or even proximity to one another?

Could one of our prized symbols of humanness—*verbal language*—be undermining our best attempts to overcome our mind's inability to remain focused? Is it possible we've outgrown the boundaries imposed on us by words and pictures? Maybe we are ready to "speak in Energy, Light & Information," an approach designed to bring us into a highly coherent universal exchange. Reconnective Healing is not only a language unto itself, it's also the Rosetta Stone, *the spiritual key* to humanity's new Universal language of the cosmos.

The Observer and the Observed

Imagine having a dream where you can observe yourself from a third-party perspective. Perhaps you're walking out of a room and see yourself from behind, or you're hovering over a scene and see yourself interacting with others. Most, if not all of us, have experienced this perspective in a dream or other state of consciousness to some degree or other.

What are the common threads throughout these experiences? A) We don't need our physical eyes the way we might in our four-dimensional earthly existence; and B) We're able to observe ourselves from a new aspect of expanded dimension, unlike the limited reflection we see when looking into a mirror.

In a Reconnective Healing Experience, it's essentially the same thing. As the facilitator, you are both the observer and the observed. First, this means you're in observation. You're observing registers, feelings, facial expressions and far more. In doing so, you're observing many aspects of *reception*. There's a lot to observe. A lot more than any of us are consciously able to perceive.

Simultaneously, you're observing *yourself*. You might observe what you're feeling. New or unexpected sensations. Hot or cold. Wet or dry. Vibration or stillness. Or hot, cold, wet, dry, vibration and stillness all at the same time. In Mindful Mindlessness, you'll probably even observe unexpected ideas or thoughts appearing in your mind. You'll likely find yourself in a place where you can be in silence, receivership, peace, nonjudgment and presence. And there'll be a high likelihood of visual perceptions, auditory, olfactory, emotional and more. Now you are both the observer of the recipient and the observer of yourself, also in reception. It's *now*. It's in the *eternal* now. The *infinite* now. It's prior to the thinking mind. It's prior to time itself. Before the thinking mind perceives everything or anything in the dual illusion of subject/object—in this example, the observer and the observed—there is only oneness. You are not the subject *or* the object, the observer *or* the observed. You are the subject *and* the object, the observer *and* the observed. **You are observation itself.**

When you experience this profound sense of oneness, *it's you in total ease. The experience doesn't precede awareness, awareness precedes the experience. Awareness reveals all experience.* You are neither directing nor attempting to determine the outcome with intentions. As the experience unfolds, you are existing in pure beingness. Quoting writer Rupert Spira, "You are the open, empty, allowing presence of Awareness, in which the objects of the body, mind and world appear and disappear, with which they are known and, ultimately, out of which they are made. Just notice that and be that, knowingly."

BECOMING THE HEALING BECOMES YOU

Many people waste enormous amounts of time and energy creating intentions and intention checklists to attract what they want or feel they need in their life. There is little accountability when we create an intention. There is a high level of accountability, however, when we place our attention somewhere truly and purely, then patiently watch while it takes shape. Hyperanalytical people will never do that. To them it feels far too uncertain to place their attention on something, surrender and passively watch, allowing it to appear and take its own form. The attachment to the thought of doing this and the possibility of not getting precisely what they want is a huge deterrent for them. As an example, if they want love, the concept of allowing themself to simply *become* love and hence attract their perfect mate, instead of trying to *design* their perfect mate in precise detail, is far too frightening an option; it feels risky, fraught with uncertainty. In truth, it's anything *but* that. The challenge faced by the hyperanalytical in approaching Reconnective Healing is that the RH requires letting go of the false sense of control they have grown used to. To heal, to truly be a healer, you have to let go of that false sense of control to *become the healing itself.* For it is only in letting go and receiving that *the perfect healing comes into being.*

This is the gift of the Mindful Mindlessness of the Reconnective Healing Experience, it is the ultimate opportunity for the mind to take a break from thinking while our undiluted essence more comfortably expresses *ITs* true nature.

So forgive yourself and enjoy your innate comedic sense and timing if, when you read this quote by Vincent Van Gogh, "I put my heart and my soul into my work, and have lost my mind in the process ... " your inner irreverent comic chimes in with "not to mention an ear, Vincent. Not to mention an ear."

The Reconnective Healing frequencies interact with us much the way the energy within a single atom of a seed helps crack open its seed coat to bring the nascent flower to fruition, in perfect latency and pure potential. From the Before-Beyond into the birth of all experience, we reclaim awareness, that perfect, timeless part of ourselves, always whole and complete.

Here's a quick review of some of the points in this chapter before we move into the exercise:

We're not only more than our thoughts and our physical bodies, we *exist* in an organization beyond what our minds and thoughts can perceive. *The Reconnective Healing Intelligence is prior* to thought, *prior* to mind, *prior* to time. We find ourselves in quiescence and coherence the moment we interact with these frequencies as they do not engage with the thinking mind.

We discussed the value of being consciously aware of That Which Is "as it is being fulfilled" and that the point of engagement with Energy, Light & Information exists somewhere *prior* to our thoughts, *prior* to our thinking mind, in the Before-Beyond and therefore in the background of all known experience. The moment we start intending, directing, controlling, expecting or predicting outcomes, our receptivity to infinite potential diminishes and becomes obscured. Knowledge is a collection of steps that lead us to a jumping-off point where we may enter into knowingness—a fieldless, stateless, pure consciousness/awareness.

We learned the Reconnective Healing frequencies interrupt negative messaging and allow self-sabotaging programs to vanish and not return. It's an interchange where *your healing becomes the awareness of your wholeness.*

We reviewed the distinction between Instinct vs. Intuition. Your instinct is your *instantaneous and unquestioning knowingness.* It is *prior* to thought. Intuition is learned and, to varying degrees, permeated with and clouded by thought and opinion. With Reconnective Healing, you're not required to be cognitively involved in the process and it's best that you aren't. We are not attempting to heal any one particular *thing ... it's neither your job nor your highest purpose to do so.* We do not *send* the healing, we *receive* it, we *become* it—and our very presence *accelerates and expands* it. A healing can happen anywhere we are. Thus, through our *attention*—not our *intention*—we become a timeless participant in healing. We are ready to "speak in Energy, Light & Information," an approach designed to bring us into a highly coherent universal exchange. You are not the subject *or* the object, you are the subject *and* the object, the observer *and* the observed. Ultimately, you are observation itself and, thus, you are Oneness.

Experience doesn't precede awareness, awareness precedes experience. Awareness reveals all experience.

It is only in letting go and receiving that *the perfect healing comes into being.*

Exercise 4:
Free-Floating in the Frequencies

Before we begin this exercise, we suggest that if you have Eric's first book, *The Reconnection: Heal Others, Heal Yourself,* reread the exercises in chapter 19,

"Finding the Energy." If you don't have the book, here is a small portion of the chapter as it relates to this exercise:

The Floating Exercise

The next exercise you will want to do is called Floating. Imagine that the room in which you're standing is filled with water up to the lower part of your chest. Starting with your hands and arms in normal anatomical position*, allow them to float up to the water's surface. Feel their buoyancy as the water supports them. Also, allow yourself to feel the surface tension of the water lightly supporting the palms of your hands. While there, notice the various sensations you experience. When you're working with a client on your table, this is one of the ways in which you'll be able to establish a reception. This will, in most people, initiate demonstration of their registers (involuntary physical responses which are often visible).

Now, let's begin this exercise by introducing some new dimensions into it. To begin, stand comfortably with your feet apart, a shoulder's width distance, and allow your hands to feel as if they are floating approximately waist high on the surface of the water, palms down. Feel them floating, let them drift. If you feel so inclined, imagine small, gentle undercurrents in the water and see in what direction they push, pull or guide your hands. Pay particular attention to the sensations you may feel in your palms and allow your hands to move where they are led. If you aren't feeling or noticing them being led anywhere, that's fine too. Just allow them to remain where they are.

Next, we're going to introduce another layer to our exploration. Think back, way back, to a toy that was first introduced to the public in 1971, the *Weeble.* For those of you who may not be familiar with what the Weeble is, take a moment and google it. It's worth seeing the visual before we continue. Their tagline was "Weebles wobble but they don't fall down." If you're not from the United States, you will probably recognize Weebles once you see their picture. Before we get started, we suggest you do this exercise very gently so that you, like the Weeble,

---

* *As taught in* The Reconnection, *this is the position your hands automatically assume when your arms and hands are hanging by your sides when you're not conscious of them.*

also don't fall down! If you need to do this in a seated or other position, feel free to modify along the way to suit your comfort, balance and other needs.

With the palms of your hands now floating on the surface of the water, hold your hands somewhat still and in a comfortable relationship to or distance from your body. Gently lock your knees and rock side-to-side. As you do this, allow your ankles to be your main pivot point and feel the surface of the water as it lightly glides underneath the surface of your palms. Gently pivot from your ankles, experimenting with the lateral side-to-side movement, then play with a forward-and-back movement, later followed by playing with a circular movement. Notice how the different movements provide variation in the way the water feels as it moves underneath your palms. Once you feel comfortable and at home with this, let's add another variable. For a sensory understanding of what we are about to do, let's first play a little with sensory recall from normal daily life.

Most of us have stood on an escalator before, and most of us have rested our hand on the handrail while we were riding the escalator. Not all of us, however, may have noticed that, more often than not, the handrail moves at a slightly different speed than the steps. If you pay close attention, you'll find that although you and the hand that's resting on the handrail are moving in the same direction, your hand may feel as if it's being pulled at a slightly faster rate than your body. We would like you to intentionally employ this awareness, this *sense memory,* here.

To do this, float your hands again on the surface of the water. As you pivot from your ankles to the left, allow your hands to glide to the left at a slightly faster speed than your body is moving. Then pivot to the right and allow your hands to glide to the right at a slightly faster pace than your body pivots. Bring your awareness to the sensation of your hands and body moving in the same direction yet at these two different speeds simultaneously. Then do the same thing forward and back. In other words, as you pivot forward, allow your hands to glide forward at a slightly faster speed. Now do the same thing in the other direction as you pivot back.

Next, as you pivot forward and back, allow your hands to move more circularly. Then repeat while pivoting side-to-side. Your hands can move circularly together with each other, then allow them to move independently of each other—maybe move your right hand clockwise while your left hand moves counterclockwise. You may even want to experiment with changing the angle or tilt of your hands while you do this, allowing them to feel half submerged in the water, as if they are pushing against the water itself.

Let's add another dimension to our game. You may have noticed that while you've been doing this, your head has naturally begun to tilt one way or the other and your eyes have begun to angle off to one side, as well as drift a bit upward or downward. Let's increase our active awareness level by intentionally implementing these additional concepts. Tilt your head in any direction you like and allow your eyes to drift off, left or right and up or down. Explore what this boost of "active listening" or active awareness adds to your experience! And feel free to play with this throughout your day to see how it complements your daily level of awareness, your *multidimensional* awareness (although you might not want to do this in crowded places for reasons that, if not already apparent to you, will probably soon become so if you do!).

Before we move onto the next chapter, know this: As you allow *IT* to flow into your life, you're going to receive many new gifts. And not always the ones you may have anticipated, as often these will be gifts beyond your imagination. One of the main gifts bestowed by Mindful Mindlessness is *certainty even in the midst of extreme chaos.*

This truly beautiful and inexplicable anomaly introduces us to a new understanding of our greatest role yet: the catalyst for healing!

1. What did I learn from this chapter?
2. What did I discover from this exercise?
3. What ideas are new to me?
4. What ideas are different than I might have thought?
5. What ideas am I now considering, contemplating?
6. Which ideas feel the most natural to me?

7. Which ideas or concepts do I have the most difficulty with or find the greatest challenge in accepting?

8. Which ideas or concepts do I have the most difficulty with or find the greatest challenge in understanding?

9. Which of my previous beliefs and ideas do I find the greatest challenge in releasing and letting go of?

10. Which ideas and concepts do I find the most freeing and empowering?

11. What has my willingness to not know already allowed me to discover? To become?

12. What might my present willingness to not know allow me to discover in the future? To become?

Please respond to the above with your thoughts, possible answers, explanations, ideas, etc., to the best of your ability.

If you don't know how to answer some of the questions above or just don't have the words, we've designed a fill-in-the-blanks model below to help you.

1. I'm not sure I know, but if I did know, the answer might be _____

2. I don't quite have the words to explain this, but if I did have the words, they might be _____

3. I don't quite have the words to describe this, but if I did have the words, they might be_____

CHAPTER 5

THE GIFT OF THE COHERENT CATALYST

*"A ... catalyst has the ability to spark significant and sustainable
changes, inspire possibilities and accelerate results."*

— *Vishwas Chavan,*

*Vishwasutras: Universal Principles for Living:
Inspired by Real-Life Experiences*

As physical embodiments of energy, human beings are essentially organic
pieces of matter composed of organized atoms, and yet the human brain allows
us to be so much more. It gives us the ability to cognitively experience, reflect
upon and interpret our lives.

But does that mean, as you're reading this book, you're cognitively creating an experience that isn't real, that doesn't exist? Is this all a fabrication of
your mind, a matrix or a virtual reality? More likely you will discover that this
book is a catalyst to opening doorways that give you access to what has been
previously unnoticed or inaccessible.

A catalyst is generally considered to cause, precipitate and/or accelerate activity between two or more persons or things. It's an impetus, incentive, motiva-
tion, stimulant, agitator, enzyme, impulse, incitement, incendiary, reactant,
synergist, radical stimulus, spark plug ... it is *inspiration.*

A conduit is generally thought of as a channel—a pipeline, an aque-
duct or a conductor. Suffice it to say, a conduit is a carrier or delivery system
in one or more forms. In our context, this infinite combination of *Energy,*

Light & Information is the conduit. Through the *awareness* of our observation, we function as a catalyst for interplay. As a catalyst in the presence of this conduit and what it brings, you allow for the revealing of a healing that has not previously been evident in that person's life, often not even consciously entertained. Within this dynamic, being the catalyst and the inspiration are really interchangeable. So think of it this way: The conduit is the delivery system for the healing and the catalyst brings the gift of healing into ultimate fruition. The Reconnective Healing Experience, then, is the catalytic event.

When we receive the murmur, a more highly organized, more highly intelligent and coherent resonance forms in our cells, tissues, DNA, the energetic field surrounding us as well as in our extrinsic reality. In this relationship, whether we're the healing facilitator or recipient, we individually develop, yield and reveal our own personal healing dynamic. This may be a visible physical healing, new levels of awareness, accelerated life progress in our daily life or pure certainty amid seemingly absolute chaos.

When you are receiving or facilitating this experience, you as the catalyst/ inspiration are interacting with the conduit of pure awareness. It is here that the frequencies are powering the two of you into a gorgeous crescendo and *all multidimensional possibilities are realizable.* The coherence occurs in a brilliant dance of inspiration, with each of you receiving immeasurably more than you would as individuals in that moment: more balance, harmony, flow, resonance and vibration necessary for your profound well-being. In this exchange, which could not happen by means of a cognitive process, the greatest good for your existence begins to align at a level beyond thought or "reason." So if someone suggests to you that this isn't reasonable, you can, with all certainty, smile at them knowingly and nod your head in agreement. Either they'll get it, or they'll get it later.

This resulting harmony is designed specially and especially for you. To sum this up: *IT* knows where to go and what to do. You simply have to, figuratively speaking, say *yes!* and get out of the way. The frequencies will have perfectly orchestrated unique and personalized experiences and effects for all. Energy, Light & Information is a pure wisdom with the power of discernment unimpeded by human concepts of judgment, right or wrong; wisdom that shares itself and imbues within us the capacity to become our very own heal-ing ... Healing itself.

Did You Hear the One About Incoherence? I'm Not Sure I Understood It.

During the last two decades, coherence has become a buzz word that has made its way into the popular lexicon. Yet to better understand being a catalyst in the world of healing, let's look a bit more deeply at the idea of coherence.

Everywhere we teach in the world, no matter the location or language, people from all walks of life want to learn more about coherence. Tom Atlee at the Co-Intelligence Institute describes it nicely: "Coherence is a form of wholeness. If things are coherent they fit together harmoniously." Prominent figures including Nassim Haramein, Gregg Braden, Lynne McTaggart, Dr. Joe Dispenza and so many others are investigating coherence through the lenses of neuroscience and quantum physics.

Science has managed to measure different aspects of coherence, yet coher-ence by itself does not confer full measurability. And as we know, nothing can be measured beyond that which we have the scientific equipment to do so, which is why we never knew infrared and ultraviolet light existed until we had the equipment to measure them. Coherence is really a scale, but just because something is a scale doesn't mean that scale has a measurable or detectable beginning or end.

We could easily get lost in the mathematics of coherence and waves. No need to worry, though: *We really don't want to do that any more than you want us to.* Fortunately, we're not talking about math here—*and hopefully nowhere else in this book!* We're talking about Reconnective Healing. So, once again, let's draw on the brilliant mind of Rollin McCraty, PhD, Executive Vice President and Director of Research at HeartMath Institute, for his definition of coherence:

"Coherence implies order, structure, harmony and alignment within systems and among systems (across systems or subsystems) ... coherence also implies the possibility of embedding great amounts of information or intelligence in coherent activities, events, signals or waveforms."

The key to McCraty's definition is that greater amounts of information or intelligence can be transferred through waveforms. In Reconnective Healing, we have our own *simpler* definition of coherence:

Coherence is our natural state when there isn't interference.
It is the presence or qualities of peace, grace and ease.

Interference can mean the pain of the past or anxiety of the future or focusing on lack, want, hurt, suffering or any other aspect of human drama that takes us out of the present moment and into a fearful state of mind. The thoughts and analyses of our brain can create a lot of interference and static. And like trying to tune into a radio station, the more interference present, the less signal (or information) you might pick up. Similarly with Reconnective Healing, the more interference we experience, the less information we may allow ourselves to cognizantly pick up. Notice, however, that we said *cognizantly* pick up. Yes, we receive the information. But if we're not cognizant of it, we don't experience it to its fullest.

In a 1962 interview, Bob Dylan once said, "The songs are there. They exist all by themselves just waiting for someone to write them down." Clearly he was alluding to this interaction.

Most artists, writers and musicians talk about the space wherein their conscious mind disappears and they become an open channel, a vessel through which creative energies freely flow.

In a Reconnective Healing exchange, the catalyst being the inspiration is an active role and identity. When we become the inspiration, our tissues, our DNA, our heart, our biophotons—our essence and our entire being for that matter—become inspirational consciousness, Energy, Light & Information for the person we're working with, the person next door and for all living beings.

As the catalyst, you are reconnecting the whole of Healing itself. You are reconnecting all the gifts of all healing protocols, all that are brought via the world's known energy healing methods, all that were brought through those that may have been forgotten, all that will be brought through those not yet known and infinitely more beyond that. We serve as a universal common denominator, allowing all to communicate, receive and interact. In a very real way, you're sharing a contagion of love and light with the world.

The Catalyst As Inspirational Impetus

"Aspire to inspire before you expire."

—*Eugene Bell, Jr.*

There are so many layers of perspective to the above statement. It is the catalyst that inspires things to take place, to occur at higher, greater or enhanced speeds and/or levels. Yet to inspire, as in to *inhale* or *breathe in,* and to expire, as in to *exhale* or *breathe out,* are functions of a conduit, i.e., our nostrils function as bidirectional conduits for the air we breathe in and out. The beauty of life-sustaining oxygen flows in, and life-sustaining (to plants) carbon dioxide flows out. So the concept of inspiration as it relates more mechanically to breathing is one of a conduit, and yet the presence of oxygen itself, and what it does in the body in many ways, although not *technically* classified as such, is a catalyst for allowing body functions to optimize. Hence breathing is both a conduit and catalyst-related activity. So, although on one hand you must inspire to expire, on the other hand, if you don't inspire, you may very well expire—in a very different sense of the word—a bit sooner than you may have intended! Therefore, as Eugene Bell, Jr., suggests, we would definitely aspire to inspire.

Perhaps when you think of the word *inspire,* you think of being infused with new energy, unbounded joy, a surge of creativity or part of the simple, beautiful and vital act of breathing. Inspiration, though, becomes even more fascinating when viewed through the prism of Reconnective Healing.

Consider these first seven entries for "inspire" on *dictionary.com.*

1. To fill with an animating, quickening, or exalting influence;
2. To produce or arouse (a feeling, thought, etc.);
3. To fill or affect with a specified feeling, thought, etc.;
4. To influence or impel;
5. To animate, as an influence, feeling, thought, or the like, does;
6. To communicate or suggest by a divine or supernatural influence;
7. To guide or control by divine influence.

Most of us don't think of ourselves as an inspiration. It may feel as if it's too big of a responsibility, an honor we might not feel worthy of. To be the inspiration may sound so self-serving and self-aggrandizing that we think to ourselves, *I could never be an inspiration,* and we become too embarrassed by the prospect to even consider it.

A personal note from Eric ...

When viewing me as "Dr. Eric Pearl," the "founder," "discoverer" or "the instrument through which Reconnective Healing chose to reveal itself," people often think of me as "the conduit." But if you've read this far in the book, you realize, of course, *that isn't true.* We know that *IT,* as an expression of Source, is the conduit. *IT* is the Intelligence and source that communicates *IT-self* in the language and frequencies of Energy, Light & Information.

When I accepted and stepped into my present role, the concept of *responsibility* arose early on: *What if the healing didn't "work?" What if I "failed" to bring about the desired results? What if I didn't have the inner catalyzing force to be ITs inspiration?* I discovered how I was allowing different aspects of my ego or personality to color or obscure the clarity of my role.

From the beginning, however, Jillian could envision no higher purpose than to accept this inspirational role of the catalyst. She could envision no higher purpose than to serve *IT,* and to support me in this endeavor. Jillian's nature is and always has been of selfless love and service. This is one of the many beautiful things that attracted me to her from the beginning and that I will always love about her.

Everyone's role—yours, ours and everybody else's—is to reveal our essence. This is our soul's force, which every one of us embodies: the vital connective tissue allowing each of us to be in our awareness of Oneness.

BECOMING AWARE OF AWARENESS

Let's now consider the nature of awareness. If you look at a tulip, you see a long, graceful stem growing upward topped with delicate, colorful petals to form the *flower.* Upon closer inspection, you see more of the tulip's parts: a stamen and pistil, indicating that it's both male and female. You would also observe its sepal, style, ovary, perhaps even some small insects who make their home in it and much more. How did that simple tulip unfold from a mere stem into something much greater? Through awareness.

The moment you direct awareness onto a fully realized tulip, the tulip's essence touches something in *your* essence—and you don't have to think about how or why the tulip moved you. Your awareness inspires it and it inspires you.

We immerse ourselves in the experience.

Here is the key to the inherent gravitational pull of Reconnective Healing. Almost at once, we find ourselves at the infinite starting point that is the end point—or the *endless* point, the Before-Beyond from which all experiences arise. Experiences we observe for their ephemeral beauty and transient qualities. Experiences that come and go while we steadfastly maintain our infinite connection.

But we are not the *sum* of these experiences: *We are their source.*

By contrast, brain-training's approach operates in the reverse. Its starting point is to try to trick our thinking into becoming what we *intend* to manifest. In other words, directing the experience to generate an intended result.

Welcome to the new physics. We indeed know that energy creates matter. Your thinking creates endless possibilities, as long as *you* keep thinking of them. But this can prove to be a quite exhausting approach.

Two points about brain training:

1. It's a lot of work
2. It requires endless maintenance

Two points about Reconnective Healing:

1. It requires no work
2. It requires no maintenance other than awareness

Whether it's the scent of a tulip (Yes, Virginia, some tulip varieties *do* have fragrances!), the melody of a piece of music, the brushstroke in a painting or the exhilarating essence of someone you love wafting through you, an instantaneous exchange takes place. That's inspiration.

In summation: The gift of the catalyst in coherence enables us to understand and experience ourselves as *IT*s inspiration, and that inspiration itself is our most coherent state of being. As an individual flame, as a part of the collective flame, this is our purpose. Maybe as a collective consciousness we are finally recognizing that we are more than our physical bodies, that something greater exists within us.

Our True Identity

We can readily discern the difference between the illusory self we present to the world and the nature of our true self within. By doing so, we allow the *essence of our being* to become the more dominant force, rather than our mind.

In this exchange, your heart starts to have a language of its own. Instead of you placing your attention on a beautiful flower, a song, a painting, a beautiful story or love, you *become* the beautiful flower, the song, the painting, the beautiful story, the love. This is what it means to be inspiration itself; the role we get to play in our everyday life: the catalyst for the conduit.

Who Does What? The Conduit, the Catalyst and the Healing Frequencies

You may find the idea of becoming a healer intriguing, even compelling. The thing is, while you may *want* to be a healer, you might also be harboring nagging doubts about yourself and how realistic the possibility of you being one is. You may find you've placed yourself in a continuous state of striving to become *good* enough, *spiritual* enough, *worthy* enough—maybe even *healthy* enough. And *striving* to become these things keeps you at a perpetual distance, in a perpetual future. It's neither your belief system nor your physical being that mediates the healings: it's your *essence*, which is *always perfect! Always* means *always*. And *always* means *now!* In other words, it's time for you to stop striving to become what you already are, to stop looking into an imaginary future for what already exists in the present ... *you!*

The Reconnective Healing Experience doesn't require that you change anything about what or who you already are. Nothing other than the illusion of self-judgment really does. To interact, you do not need to raise the frequency of your energy, nor do anything to produce results. The optimizing that comes about through the experience occurs without any prep work required. As a matter of fact, the less prep, the better. The less anticipation and the less attachment, the more freedom for this intelligence to go where it knows to go and do what it knows to do best. We are each already enough just as we are. And if you've read this far in this book, this means you. Period.

What Do Healing And Playing Have To Do With Each Other?

For the newcomer, and even the seasoned energy healer, using the word *play* in the context of healing can be somewhat challenging.

When we are healing someone or healing ourselves, the idea of play can appear to diminish the importance of the healing process. In the beginning, as a new student, we may enter the healing session with a desire for control and precision, to effect explicit changes. We want to feel we are *doing, doing, doing*... and doing it *right*. If we are myopically focused on healing a part of ourselves as well, the control meter swings even higher. The drumroll moment happens when our awareness of *IT* amplifies and we find ourselves instantly and inexplicably ushered into a timeless interplay with the unknown, the not yet known, the unknowable, the unseen, the unseeable and, ultimately, the *new known* of just being! And the drumroll, along with everything else, recedes into silence.

If, however, you can remain the detached observer, *if* you can remain in that childlike state of receiving, engaging in the healing process at this level becomes play.

To experience the art of play in Reconnective Healing is as unforgettable as the first time you floated in the salty water of the ocean without using your arms or legs or gazed in wonder at a sunset sinking below the horizon or the ecstatic sensation of your first kiss. It begs us to find the balance between cosmic curiosity and our mind's unquenchable thirst to know the how and why of everything. The questions of how and why may be important in spurring societal evolution onward, but they also give the mind permission to create the illusion of separateness. When that illusion falls away, distance falls away. And when distance falls away, all that's left is Oneness.

Let's take a moment and review some of the points in this chapter before we move into the exercise. See how many of these points you remember.

In this chapter we explored opening doorways that give you access to what has been previously unnoticed or inaccessible, our role as catalyst and inspiration, and the difference between that and being a conduit. We recognized Reconnective Healing as the reunification of all communication protocols in the field of healing and that receiving a "murmur" allows for a more highly organized, intelligent and coherent resonance to form in our cells, tissues, DNA, energetic field and our extrinsic reality, and that this brings order, structure, alignment and harmony to our lives. We discussed experiencing as well as *being* certainty in seeming chaos, coherence as our natural state, facilitating healing as naturally as breathing in and breathing out, becoming aware of awareness, the starting point as both the endpoint and the endless point. We revealed to ourself that it's neither our belief system nor our physical being that mediates healing: It's our *essence*, which is *always perfect!* We realized that in healing, the less cerebral planning and intentional preparation, the better. And, simply put, we discovered that remaining the unattached observer in a childlike state of expectancy and receiving is a true gift for everyone involved.

So now, let's glide into part one of a two-part exercise called Eye See You!

Exercise 5:
Eye See You: Part 1

You're now ready to advance to a different kind of exercise, one more specifically involving your eyes! Although Reconnective Healing is not about trying to bring about or elicit certain responses, there is definitely a level of *responsiveness* that at times shows up in *some* ways, and at other times in *other* ways. It's the unexpected that helps maintain our fascination and curiosity, and it's our fascination that helps keep us in presence.

For this exercise, you can do the first part by yourself. It comes with a caution, however: *Do not do this while there are other people around or they may consider you to be loony.*

To begin, hold one hand open, palm facing you and fingers spread apart about as far as you comfortably can. Hold your fingers open and stare into your palm. Just stare at it. Stare at it and allow whatever sensations that may come about to arrive in your palm. Notice your fingers. Notice if and when they start to move. Usually one finger starts, then more join in. Just observe, notice and see what comes about for you. Now do it with your other hand. Each hand tends to have its own unique kind of response.

You may have shown subtle movement of the fingers, or may have seen larger, more obvious and demonstrable movements. *But let's take this to the next level,* because this may possibly become one of the more intriguing exercises in the field of Reconnective Healing you may have yet experienced. Again, we want to take this moment to reinforce our recommendation that you read *The Reconnection* and watch *The Portal,* the Reconnective Healing Level I Online Course, to get the most out of these exercises and experiences. But even if you haven't done either yet, these exercises will most likely demonstrate surprisingly well for you.

So here comes the big leap. *We know you're ready!* One thing, though—this part of the exercise requires a volunteer to work with you. We know that the idea of finding someone for you to practice this exercise on may make you feel like groaning. But take it from us, once you do this, you will more than likely be so surprised, inspired and exhilarated with what you observe, as well as what you hear from the other person, that you will quickly find yourself looking for the next person you can do this with. So, buck up. Here we go.

Grab a friend, a family member, a friend's friend, a lover, an ex-lover or a total stranger. It doesn't matter whether they believe in this or not. The main requirement is that they are breathing and are willing to lie down comfortably on a massage table on their back, along the foot or side of a bed, a sofa or even sit in a chair. Then ask them to allow their eyes to close and to let go.

While your volunteer is lying or sitting down, eyes closed and relaxed, you may bravely take your hands and place them behind your back. That's right. We're going to work without our hands. We're going to work with our eyes!

First, choose one of their eyes and stare at it for six seconds or so. Now look at the other eye and stare at it for approximately the same length of time. Return to the first eye and repeat. Then the other. As you move from eye to eye, you may opt to do this either by simply shifting your gaze or by choosing to implement the Weeblelike pivoting we spoke of in our chapter 4 exercise. Both bring about interesting registers and are slightly different experiences. You will want to play, experiment and find what's most interesting. You may choose to work in different ways at different times and with different people.

Now, slowly pick up speed just a bit, moving back and forth, switching from the person's right eye to their left eye and back again. For example, stay focused on each eye for approximately two seconds, then one second each, then move from eye to eye even faster. Observe how this affects the speed of their eye registers (involuntary movements) as well as the intensity. Then stop and take a pause.

Next we want you, in silent focus, to slightly lean in or bend forward until your eyes are directly above your partner's lips. Remain standing so you are at least two feet or approximately half a meter away from the person. (This is not meant to become a physically intimate moment!) Fix your gaze so you are staring directly at where their lips meet, maybe even imagining that you can see their two front teeth. Continue to stare. Watch. Observe. Witness. Experiment with standing absolutely still and gently pivoting in silence. Watch for muscle movement. A separation of the lips. Then maybe more active movements of the lips. You may possibly see a rippling of the muscles around the mouth or chin. Observe what follows. This is a door-opening moment. Allow the door to open in its own manner and its own time. You will see different responses in different people. Most of these responses will be intriguing and compelling. Stay curious.

1. What did I learn from this chapter?
2. What did I discover from this exercise?
3. What ideas are new to me?
4. What ideas are different than I might have thought?
5. What ideas am I now considering, contemplating?
6. Which ideas feel the most natural to me?
7. Which ideas or concepts do I have the most difficulty with or find the greatest challenge in accepting?

8. Which ideas or concepts do I have the most difficulty with or find the greatest challenge in understanding?

9. Which of my previous beliefs and ideas do I find the greatest challenge in releasing and letting go of?

10. Which ideas and concepts do I find the most freeing and empowering?

11. What has my willingness to not know already allowed me to discover? To become?

12. What might my present willingness to not know allow me to discover in the future? To become?

Please respond to the above with your thoughts, possible answers, explanations, ideas, etc., to the best of your ability.

If you don't know how to answer some of the questions above or just don't have the words, we've designed a fill-in-the-blanks model below to help you.

1. I'm not sure I know, but if I did know, the answer might be

    _____

2. I don't quite have the words to explain this, but if I did have the words, they might be _____

3. I don't quite have the words to describe this, but if I did have the words, they might be_____

CHAPTER 6
THE GIFT OF DISTANCE

"When there is no more separation between 'this' and 'that,'
it is called the still-point of the Tao. At the still point in the
center of the circle one can see the infinite in all things."

—Zhuangzi

No matter the context, the word "distance" can often have a negative connotation. For instance, if we think of distance in regard to spaces or places, it's the space *between* two things, a state of separateness, remoteness, a vast expanse or the time it takes to get from point A to point B, exemplified in the classic persistent question of the inevitably bored child on a long family drive: "Are we there yet?"

If we think about distance in terms of a relationship between two people, it may suggest a physical or emotional separation or that one person may be pulling away from the other. Viewed this way, distance may generate fear and insecurity.

As clearly evident in Reconnective Healing, however, physical distance becomes the *disappearance* of distance, physical separation becomes the *disappearance* of separation. Put differently, it's the collapsing of distance into Oneness or unity. The dissolving of otherness. Regardless of which of these descriptions resonates most with you, they all allow for greater love.

This *presence,* found through the disappearance of distance, is a powerful and central characteristic of the Reconnective Healing Experience, a basic truth, an absolute and enduring property. The experience of Reconnective Healing reveals the *illusion* of distance; reveals the *illusion* that distance exists, that distance *is*; reveals it to be an *illusion* based upon the illusion of space and time reinforced by fear, in particular, our fear of separation.

Reconnective Healing is an anomaly in that its reception becomes *stronger* with distance. For at least a period of time, and sometimes into perpetuity, anomalies are generally unexplainable — *until they become explainable.* That is, until science catches up enough to describe or measure the observation. So, while we can't tell you *precisely* where the Reconnective Healing frequencies come from ... (although it's been rumored they come from a very small town in New Jersey up near the George Washington Bridge ...), we do know they exist prior to the dimensions of height, width, depth and time—the dimensions we experience through our senses.

Countless researchers and quantum physicists have and continue to study Reconnective Healing yet remain puzzled when it comes to figuring out the mechanics of the interactions. This has prompted them and us to ask the following questions:

- *Where else in the universe does "energy" behave in this manner?*
- *What else in the universe doesn't diminish with space or time but instead strengthens and expands with it?*
- *What else in the universe expands instead of contracting simply by virtue of you opening yourself up to receive it?*

Love. Love is the answer. It knows no bounds. Beyond love, and within the laws of the physical universe, we don't know of any other energies that behave in such a manner or possess such properties.

Here we have one of the many ways the Reconnective Healing frequencies seem to turn physics' mathematical equations of energy upside down and inside out. This tends to both fascinate and boggle the minds of the physicists who attend our programs.

Loving Detachment vs. Fear of Detachment

There's another Gift bestowed by Distance—a new paradigm we refer to as loving detachment.

When facilitating Reconnective Healing from the understanding that we are all one, we are freed from attempting to *become* one with the recipient. In this way otherness simply dissolves and therefore gives us permission to *witness* that we are love, in and as our very presence. Everywhere. Simultaneously. In this zone of loving detachment we find new strength, fortification and authenticity. In our three-way interconnectedness with the Reconnective Healing frequencies there is no separation. Thereisnoseparation.

Imagine attending a party with the love of your life. You can be on two different sides of the room, yet you always know you are both present as one. You can see your partner even when not looking in their direction. You can feel them even though you may be half a room away. You can "hear" their thoughts and know they can hear yours. Whether we are aware of it or not, we are one consciousness. Always. And in all ways. As Albert Einstein said, "Our separation from each other is an optical illusion of consciousness."

How we experience Reconnective Healing's concept of distance might have something to do with its anomalous characteristics. Loving detachment changes the way we view everything and everyone. There is no risk of loss, and there is no risk of losing *IT*s love. In this magical liberated state, we experience the connectivity of infinite love. Not love mired in emotional attachment. Instead, a love that expresses itself without words. A Oneness wherein all may transcend their perceived limitations. Where it is understood that confines are only the illusion of a limited imagination.

In this *new known,* we are able to enter into and embrace *Distance Reconnective Healing.* With the integrated new known, some people might assume this is the strongest form of Reconnective Healing because there are more miles between person A and person B. However, those who have participated in our live training programs have seen the emancipating effect of how distance dramatically increases and intensifies the experience for both people in the same room. This does not mean that distance healing—healing sessions where the practitioner and the client are not in the same room, city or even part of the world—are stronger or more powerful. Jillian and I love to facilitate Reconnective Healing Distance Sessions. They are of equal strength. And the more we release attachment to trying to make one stronger or otherwise of preferable value, the more we experience and receive. They are different, just as every session is different. And simultaneously they are quite the same. But we should not equate this emancipation with *better.* With or without the perceived element of distance, everything is touching and nothing is touching, and we experience this as the loving detachment of Oneness.

The key to our attachment to distance—or lack thereof—is a compassionate instinct within us to want to be in *hands-on* mode when facilitating a healing for someone. It seems that physical proximity can trigger the ego into *doing* and *sending* mode, rather than *allowing* and *receiving* mode. In many healing modalities, healers are taught to touch or keep their hands close to a person's body or to move no farther than a given distance such a few inches away. A practitioner coming from a massage or physical therapy background might say, "Why do I want to be hands-off the body? I won't be physically connecting with the person." Often people confuse not physically connecting with not connecting.

What many people don't realize is the unconscious message beneath this perspective is fear. That's because instructing someone to touch or stay in close proximity implies that the energy may otherwise dissipate, lose its potency or possibly not even arrive at the client. This message can also introduce fear and distrust into a healing process with the potential to manifest the illusion of what the facilitator and/or recipient may be most in fear of. As a result, the practitioner begins focusing more on technique and sending rather than on what's most empowering for everyone: receiving, witnessing and presence through distance—whether inches, feet or miles—*loving detachment.*

When we become lovingly detached, we create the space to allow these frequencies to most effectively move through us.

Eric had a client who came to see him for a session in the first years of his discovering Reconnective Healing. She was continuously opening her eyes, checking on what was going on. Almost from the moment they began her session she was telling him that he was holding his hands too far away from her and to move them closer. Eric explained the dynamics of this, but she didn't want to hear it. After the session she told him that she didn't feel anything. She reiterated, "Nothing happened because you were holding your hands too far away from me," and left in a huff. She did have a healing, one that she later graciously let him know about it. She was just too focused on what she thought she should be feeling during her session to notice it at the time.

Don't confuse what someone notices with what's really happening. They are not always one and the same. To quote the Mundaka Upanishad, "In detachment lies the wisdom of uncertainty, in the wisdom of uncertainty lies the freedom from our past, from the known, which is the prison of past conditioning."

In the consciousness of loving detachment, something changes within both the healer and the recipient. An appreciation for being the healing itself, not just the healer and the healed, being witnessing itself, not just the witness and the witnessed, being observation itself, not just the observer and the observed. You are present and *presence.* This is a phenomenon similar to the "Overview Effect" reported by astronauts during spaceflight, especially when viewing Earth from orbit or from the lunar surface. It's seeing firsthand an augmented reality of who we are and where we are, a manifestation of an expanded awareness of connection and Oneness.

As far as we can tell—which is a statement in itself—we are the most evolved of species on a tiny blue planet floating through a void. Within this void, our planet happens to exist in what's called the Goldilocks Zone, or what we might lovingly refer to as Goldilocks' "optimal porridge zone" (not too hot, not too cold ... *just right!),* better known as the circumstellar habitable zone (CHZ), or simply the habitable zone.

When we look at Earth from this vantage point—just as Reconnective Healing disappears distance and dissolves otherness—boundaries, ideologies and all other differences on our planet disappear. As we allow ourselves to look at the whole of our existence from this vantage point, we discover that conflict disappears and we instantly realize that *everything*, and therefore *everyone*, is indeed touching, and that simultaneously *nothing*, and therefore *no one*, is touching. Healing courtesy of a visit to the Goldilocks Zone! Within this vastness, distance and separation are, in fact, not real, and we exist in, and as, Oneness.

As we give ourselves permission to live within this greater realization we no longer feel moored to Earth. This enhanced perspective indelibly changes our relationship to everything around us. It even impacts our understanding of the natural laws that govern us, including the laws of gravity. The immense changes we experience are internal, external and eternal.

In a Reconnective Healing Experience, this is what happens when you receive *IT:* You move into an awareness of infinite existence and allow yourself to become the catalyst and create space for *IT* to be the greater shared part of who and what you already are. The intelligence of this Energy, Light & Information shifts your deepest understanding of the laws you unconsciously adhere to and abide by. *IT* becomes the greater part of you and everyone you share your existence with. *IT* becomes your new vibrational reality. And in this you allow the infinite to experience itself as *you*. You enter into this very clear experience, a lovingly detached omnidimensionality, and you come to realize the actual value of your being's inner essence. The more the illusory concept of distance disappears, the more you expand.

As you allow for this quiescent expansion, you find you've gotten out of the way of your limited human, conscious, educated mind because you're no longer trying to intend or direct. And in the process, your ego has allowed itself to leave the room.

The experience and the healing may have *nothing to do with your cognizant awareness*. You don't need to consciously know what is happening. You are only there to receive, participate, inspire, witness, observe, experience and *serve* as the limitless potential of healing.

Here's a quick review of some of the points in this chapter; then we'll jump into the exercise.

We looked at the collapsing of distance into Oneness, the disappearance of separation, the dissolving of otherness, as well as some of the perceived negative baggage the word carries. We explored Reconnective Healing as an anomaly because, among other things, reception becomes stronger with distance and doesn't dissipate with time, that the healing turns the mathematical equations of quantum physics upside down and inside out, distance becoming the disappearance of distance and separation becoming the disappearance of separation. We talked about the risk-free zone of loving detachment, that everything is touching and nothing is touching, everyone is touching and no one is touching, and we discovered freedom from trying to become one with anyone or anything. We looked at separation as an optical illusion of consciousness as stated by Einstein. We explored loving detachment and the connectivity of infinite love. We looked at the gifts of distance healing sessions and in-person healing sessions. We explored the triggers of "doing" and "sending" compared to "allowing" and "receiving." We witness fear of distance becoming the gifts of awe and wonder in distance. And we even looked into insights from the Goldilocks Zone of Healing. Most importantly, we learned that healing isn't *like* love. Healing *is* love.

Exercise 6:
Eye See You: Part 2

We're now going to repeat the Eye See You exercise from chapter 5, but with a different twist at the end of it. Let's bring you through this first part again now. Remember that although Reconnective Healing is not about trying to bring about or elicit certain responses, there is definitely a level of *responsiveness* that at times shows up in *some* ways, and at other times in *other* ways. It's the unexpected that helps maintain our fascination and curiosity, and it's our fascination that helps keep us in presence.

You can do the first part of the exercise by yourself. (But if you do this in public and people stare, we suggest you avoid the temptation to make crazy faces back at them as it might appear to confirm their suspicion.) Now, just as before, hold one hand open, palm facing you and fingers spread apart about as far as you comfortably can. Sometimes simply extending your pinky finger will bring about an appropriate pull in your palm to help you become more aware of the sensation of the Reconnective Healing frequencies. Hold your fingers open and stare into your palm. Just stare into it. Stare at it and allow whatever sensations that come about to arrive in your palm. Notice your fingers. Notice if and when they start to move. Usually one finger may start, then more will join in. Observe, notice and see what comes about for you. Now repeat that with your other hand. Each hand tends to have its own unique kind of response as you probably noticed the first time we did this.

You may have seen subtle movement of your fingers, or you might have seen larger, more obvious movements once again.

Now this is the part that requires a volunteer to partner up with, so wrangle up a willing participant. It doesn't matter whether they believe in this or not. Sometimes it's more fun if they don't. Ask them to lie down comfortably on a massage table on their back or along the foot or side of a bed, a sofa or to sit in a chair. Then ask them to close their eyes and let go.

While your volunteer is lying or sitting down, eyes closed and relaxed, take your hands and place them behind your back. First, choose one of their eyes and stare at it for six seconds or so. Now look at the other eye and stare at it for approximately the same length of time. Return to the first eye and repeat. Then the other. As you move from eye to eye, you may opt to do this either by simply shifting your gaze or you may choose to implement the Weeblelike pivot. Both bring about interesting registers and provide slightly different experiences for you and your volunteer. You will want to play, experiment and explore. Some things work differently at different times and with different people.

Begin now to increasingly pick up speed, moving back and forth, switching from the person's right eye to their left eye and back again. For example, stay focused on each eye for approximately two seconds, then one second each, then move from eye to eye even faster. Observe how this affects the speed of their eye registers (involuntary movements) as well as the pattern and intensity of the movements. Then stop and take a pause.

Next, in silent focus, slightly lean in or bend forward until your eyes are directly above their lips. Remain standing so you are at least two feet away from the person. Reminder: Maintain a professional distance and give them plenty of space. Now fix your gaze so you are staring directly at where their lips meet, maybe even imagining that you can see their two front teeth. Continue to stare. You might be surprised. Watch. Observe. Witness. Experiment with standing absolutely still and gently pivoting in silence. Watch for muscle movement. A separation of the lips. Then maybe more active movements of the lips. You may possibly see a rippling of the muscles around the mouth or chin. Observe what follows. Allow this door-opening moment to widen in its own manner and its own time as you observe different responses.

We are experiencing this exercise a second time now because here it becomes a lead-in to Part II: Your walk into the real world with the Reconnective Healing frequencies, or bringing the *real* world into your walk through heightened awareness. So, in silence, you are about to embark on a bit of a discovery, a miniwalkabout, a silent retreat of sorts for the next five–60 minutes, or whatever length of time feels best for you. And we strongly suggest you bring your partner on this silent walkabout with you.

Your walkabout can take you wherever you like. You may choose to explore your street or neighborhood, you may journey out to your garden or another beautiful location, notice how the fragrances of the flowers seem to sparkle inside your nose and take on new dimension, bear witness to an apparent new majesty of the trees or rediscover your own backyard as facets and aspects of it heretofore unnoticed become as clear and vivid as a morning sunrise crowning like a newborn's head from behind a mountaintop or an ocean horizon. You may even walk through a park or a beautifully landscaped area as you take in the joy and expressiveness you see in the faces of others and in the lives of this earth's creatures and inhabitants, large and small.

In silence, walk. Allow the sounds of the outside world to become simply a part of the tapestry in which you exist. Allow the sounds, whatever they are, to flow in, to flow out. Observe the colors. How do they appear to you? The same as before? Or brighter, sharper, clearer, more vibrant? Can you begin to see colors in the colors you might not have noticed before? What about the sky? Is the blue the same blue, are the clouds the same density and vibrance? The color of the grass, the smell of the air, the fragrances as they intermingle and tap you on the nose. Feel the air. Observe the people and life forms as you share this space of life with them; notice how you feel around them and how they appear to feel around you. Listen to your inner observations. Observe yourself in silence. Walk in awareness. Notice what has changed—or is it simply you who's changed? Once you return to where you started, or find a nice place to sit and settle, you may choose to discuss your observations with your partner. You might be quite surprised by their experience and observations as well.

1. What did I learn from this chapter?
2. What did I discover from this exercise?
3. What ideas are new to me?
4. What ideas are different than I might have thought?

5. What ideas am I now considering, contemplating?

6. Which ideas feel the most natural to me?

7. Which ideas or concepts do I have the most difficulty with or find the greatest challenge in accepting?

8. Which ideas or concepts do I have the most difficulty with or find the greatest challenge in understanding?

9. Which of my previous beliefs and ideas do I find the greatest challenge in releasing and letting go of?

10. Which ideas and concepts do I find the most freeing and empowering?

11. What has my willingness to not know already allowed me to discover? To become?

12. What might my present willingness to not know allow me to discover in the future? To become?

Please respond to the above with your thoughts, possible answers, explanations, ideas, etc., to the best of your ability.

If you don't know how to answer some of the questions above or just don't have the words, we've designed a fill-in-the-blanks model below to help you.

1. I'm not sure I know, but if I did know, the answer might be _____

2. I don't quite have the words to explain this, but if I did have the words, they might be _____

3. I don't quite have the words to describe this, but if I did have the words, they might be_____

CHAPTER 7

I AM... THE HEALER

"You are integral to a process that is coming in a great scope.
It will not only resonate in your life, but clearly in the lives you touch."

—*Solomon from* Solomon Speaks On Reconnecting Your Life

As we recognize that I am the healer, you are the healer, God is the healer, we allow ourselves to recognize that he, she, it, we and they, too, are the healer. Ultimately it becomes clear that I, you, he, she, it, we and they are one with God, Love and the Infinite Intelligence of the Universe. In essence, our essence and *all essence* is God, Love and the Infinite Intelligence of the Universe.

In this chapter we emphasize not the *I* of the separate self, but rather the *I* of *I Am.* The *I* of the separate self is the localization of the personality and the ego, while the *I* of *I Am* begins the illumination of our infinite existence and hence our relationship to and beingness as God, Love, the Universe, Source, Creator ... select whatever name you like, for it is only the human that cares about a name.

Rupert Spira reminds us, "The search for God is the denial of what we are. And that is blasphemy."

Being a healer is its own reward, and opportunities for it are available to everyone. It is a reward that is optimally received and experienced when we are no longer looking to supplement ourselves or the healing. For only then may we truly be the healer, and this can only be achieved when we are no longer looking to control, direct or determine the healing outcome, nor to take credit for it, nor attempt to tell the universe where to go, what to do and how to do it. As a healer, you exist in a recognition of here, everpresence and *being,* which is its own excellence, its own reward. Maybe this is what the entity we call Solomon was elucidating when he said, "You must *see* that you are a master. You must *know* that you are a master." For you are life and existence itself.

The Gift of the Healer

I am presence, I am wonder, I am innocence.
I am willing to not know and yet be in knowingness simultaneously.
I am willing to not know the form of the healing
and yet be in knowingness that it is in perfect form.
I am certainty in chaos, and the chaos in my certainty.
I am integrity, I am wisdom—not always fully expressing either
yet always a perfect expression of both.
I am impetus. I am inspiration.
I am essence.
I am consciousness, yet not self-consciousness. I am aware and awareness.
I manifest as matter and I matter.
I am vibration and I am resonance in my stillness. I am a photon. I am a proton.
I am in, I am of, and I Am.
I am my own healing and thus my own revealing, and I am simultaneously
the healing and revealing of humanity and the universe.
I am you. You are me. We Are. I Am.

—Eric Pearl & Jillian Fleer

The role of the healing facilitator requires consciousness and expanded awareness, as well as other vital attributes. The persona and qualities you bring to the equation, including nonjudgmental compassion, contribute to the totality of your *presence*.

As a Reconnective Healing practitioner proceeds into the timeless, an equation existing beyond our current languages, mathematics and metric systems arises. Let's look at this more closely. As the Healer, we are the reception of the grace and freedom that pulsate within *IT's* infiniteness. In this magnificent way, we release the illusory burden of feeling responsible for the healing result, while we simultaneously free ourselves of the part of our ego that wants to take credit for it.

In short: We no longer have to worry about establishing a specific outcome, result or response, nor about the guilt and burden we falsely assume when we don't see or recognize the outcome we tried to impose. We simply allow ourselves to fall into the quiescent, both as catalyst and witness. And because we released the idea of the healer as being separate, we assume the loving role of being observation, participation and, on a grander scale, witnessing. In this threefold role, we can only be accountable to ourselves as the vessel through which *IT* brings light and experience to the world.

We are *ITs* Instrument

To be *ITs* instrument is the true calling of the healer. We become an instrument through the ultimate gift of receiving bestowed upon us by simply having been born.

You are the song and the symphony. *But do you hear your own music?* Ideally, as the healer we seek to explore our personal healing, self-discovery and evolution to become the freedom inherent in who and what we are. Yet again and again we find ourselves wandering onto paths involving so much sustained and persistent effort that living our freedom seems unattainable. We forget that we *are* freedom, so *finding* our freedom is finding *ourself.* You are the ultimate instrument for the Reconnective Healing Frequencies. Learn how to be in tune, compose and play your melody.

Let us reiterate:

> *Being a healer is its own reward,*
> *its own accomplishment, its own consummate impeccability.*

What then may be preventing you from seeing, knowing and being?

The Reconnective Healing Experience is so simple and natural that we often talk ourselves *out* of ITs reality, *out* of what we've witnessed in another, or even *out* of what we've experienced *firsthand.* We often deny ourselves the vision to actually see ITs truth.

Today, each and every one of us has moved beyond observing just the visible, physical healings. There's so much more in this that's of value to us. On one hand, we can't get there if we limit ourselves to simply observing the physical. And yet, to move further, we need to fully embrace and acknowledge what we witness. We cannot allow ourselves to feel that we've seen it all or learned it all. Even *entertaining* that thought becomes irrefutable evidence that we haven't, and by becoming jaded in that way, we impede our life progress.

One of the highest gifts we can give ourselves is the willingness to witness the purity of innocence. The more the science and the mystery of things reveal themselves, the more we continue to evolve. Today, however, the allure of complexity prevents all too many from enjoying the incomparable benefits that come only through simplicity.

The dominant left brain is essentially interested in what can be measured. What we *cannot* quantify, we *prefer* and *feel safer* attributing to something *else* or *anything* else. Perhaps this explains why what cannot be measured may be perceived by some as "magical" and therefore considered "suspect." As Eckhart Tolle observes, "Sometimes surrender means giving up trying to understand, and becoming comfortable with not knowing."

What Is Surrender?

Usually we think of surrender as the *last* thing we might want to do, as something far from desirable or optimal. Throw in a dash of ego and suddenly it's viewed through a screen of loss with overtones of humiliation. If we contemplate it through the analogy of war or even overall competition, we think of it as defeat or failure. And let's face it, most people aren't overly excited about that. *Or, sometimes, possibly, we might want to surrender.*

Was the underlying theme in Eric's first book, *The Reconnection: Heal Others, Heal Yourself,* one of surrender? Eric's surrender? Is that what was so inspirational and touches the hearts of millions even today? Was it the recognition of me as you and you as me? Is it the ultimate desirability and reward of surrender that our egos resist and yet, once given in to, we find unfathomable reward and pleasure in? Is it the key to the freedom we thought we would gain through struggle? Is it what brings us the rewards we thought would come through power and prestige?

We are here as molecules, souls that represent surrender. Not surrender obscured by ego-driven desire, but rather the surrender that can only come through Grace with a capital "G." And then this intelligence uses us like a mosquito of contagion for good to share and spread the Reconnective Healing

Experience through the invitation of Grace—an invitation that we accepted nowhere near as regularly and consistently as we might, in retrospect, have liked, have appreciated, as would have benefitted us.

Surrender can be a challenge. One we hope to accept more and more.

The Elegant Simplicity of the Technique-Free Healer

There is a simple elegance to being a healer. It's not about the clothes you wear or the way in which you move your hands. It's not about extending your pinky as if you're about to sip an afternoon cup of tea, nor is it about attempting to mirror the grace of a gazelle or walking around as if you're wearing clouds on your feet instead of shoes. It's about your *inner* being, the harmony *of* your presence *in* your presence. It's learning to be yourself, to play yourself as the infinite instrument of experience created as *you*.

For the healer, elegance resides in the ease and simplicity of being technique-free. When you look at an individual who radiates presence, maybe an orchestra conductor at the peak of a crescendo, a dancer in midair or an athlete in peak zone play, there is no remnant of technique in their ease. Whatever technique they may have once explored, contemplated or applied has been allowed to dissolve and transmute into beingness. Any state of trying evaporates, allowing their inherent beauty and authenticity to shine through. The intrinsic truth of the healer embodies this concept, including the understanding that no special healer's clothing or accoutrements are required. Gone is the artificial focus on the external. Rather than worn on the outside, the elegance of simplicity is an effortless refinement that comes from within, from our essence; it can neither be contained nor hidden, threatened nor beguiled. It is irreducible and ineffable.

What but fear keeps us separate from the elegant embodiment of the healer? The fear that we're not good enough. The fear of our own worthiness. The fear that we may not even be worthy of being worthy. Worthy to heal. Worthy to *be* healed. What also keeps us at arm's length is the fear of how we might be perceived by others, the intertwined desire to represent ourselves as we think we *should,* and maybe even how someone *else* thinks we should. So many of us live in fear bubbles. We question whether we're deserving, we feel hesitant, awkward and insecure about tapping into a nascent, vaguely sensed capability. Fear that we might be revealed, that others might discover our *own* deep-seated insecurities.

Once we push through our fear of being revealed as an imposter, we will likely discover the truth: that our fears were unfounded and illusory all along. To love is to be vulnerable, and to share vulnerability is not weakness but the ultimate strength. Vulnerability, love's natural condition, enables the unveiling of our soul to another person's soul, and a surrendering of our illusions to a transcendent truth. As Brené Brown describes it, "Vulnerability is basically uncertainty, risk, and emotional exposure."

Vulnerability born of love enables us to embrace the level of our true nature as light and consciousness. There is no separation—just oneness, an endless wellspring of love—the highest, most coherent, purest frequency. Precisely the state of being Solomon was referring to when he said, "You must *see* that you are a master. You must *know* that you are a master."

Knowingness and vision is bestowed upon us only when we confront the enormous fear and revelation that we are not the conduit, but rather the instrument, the vessel, the catalyst; this is what we confront when we are faced with overcoming the separation or distinction between healer and healing. This is the fear that makes itself felt in what may be our single, biggest healing question: *What if the healing doesn't work?*

Many of us have chosen to enter the field of healing because of a deep desire to alleviate the pain and suffering of others—*a very noble-sounding reason!* Today, however, more and more healers are coming to recognize that *pain and suffering are not the real problems,* they are merely *indicators* of a problem signaling that something is out of balance. In other words, it's not about us addressing the pain and suffering, high-minded and virtuous as that may sound. It's about *healing Intelligence restoring balance.*

Logically this is easy enough to understand. Yet when an emotional attachment to a specific healing outcome takes over, this concept, this understanding, becomes easily obscured. Sometimes it seems to fly out the window like the proverbial baby with the bathwater, other times we throw it out the window.

Let's consider the question we brought up earlier: *What if the healing doesn't work?* We may *think* that's the question those words are asking. And those words clearly *sound* as if that's the question they're asking. Literally that's *certainly* the question being asked, yet in reality, it isn't.

The real question being asked, in fact, is: *What if I don't bring about the results that I, in my limited human perspective, think I should? What if I don't provide the results* they *desire and expect? What if their symptoms don't magically and instantaneously disappear? What if their healing doesn't look like what they* think *they want it to look like? Or doesn't look like what* I *think* I *want it to look like? In essence, what if the Intelligence of this Universe has something else in mind? Something* I *wasn't cognitively aware of when* I *was busy "intending" my cerebrally designed outcome? "Imposing" my emotionally designed outcome? And can* I, *in my perceived and self-entitled sense of omniscience, overrule that? Thankfully* I *realize that* I *wouldn't ever want to.*

This is the type of personality/ego/fear-based thinking that distracts our attention from the bigger picture of healing as one of restoring or achieving balance and leads our focus back off course to the alleviation of pain, suffering and other symptoms. Once again the ego rears its head and healing *attention* is replaced by symptom-focused *intention*. In appreciating this concept, we realize that we wouldn't ever want it to be that way. Removing symptoms isn't the same as restoring health. Restoring balance and health, however, usually includes the alleviation of symptoms.

Today, we have access to a wide range of electronic devices, therapies, interventions, over-the-counter and prescription drugs, telemedicine, a multitude of herbs, roots, teas, homeopathics, flower essences and other alternative remedies and protocols. And although we commonly classify these as alternative healing approaches, and they have many benefits, if you take a closer look, you'll probably recognize them to be symptom-based approaches, basically treatments and therapies that, more often than not, overlook the cause of the problem. We may not always think of these as such, but when we take homeopathic "A" for one annoying symptom and herbal "B" for another, when we use electronic device "C" for this pain, flower remedy "D" for that emotional discomfort (blissfully ignoring the peculiar coincidence that the flower of origin often has an oddly similar name to the symptoms you are taking it for), over-the-counter medicine "E" for sleep, "F" for nerves and "G" for skin eruptions, if we observe this objectively, the symptom-over-cause priority of many of these modes becomes quite clear.

Reconnective Healing does *not* primarily focus on the presenting symptoms. Although the *results* of receiving an RHE tend to *include* the alleviation of symptoms, that isn't the Reconnective Healing Experience's overriding purpose. Symptom alleviation is what we like to refer to as a "by the way." We hear things such as, "Ever since my Reconnective Healing Experiences, I'm waking up earlier and with more energy, my career's skyrocketing, I found true love, my kids are talking to me in a different way that I really enjoy and, oh, *by the way,* that pesky headache that I had for three month is gone," "*by the way,* that skin problem I had that runs in my family vanished overnight and hasn't returned," "*by the way,* my hip feels so good I don't need my wheelchair or walker anymore." Treating symptoms can sound alluring and sometimes be thought of as helping people on their way to being better. Yet Reconnective Healing is about something much more. More relevant, ultimately more significant. It's not only a return to a greater degree of wholeness, integrity of being and balance on all levels—the totality of which we recognize as physical, emotional, mental, spiritual health and then some—it can also thrust you onto a course of greater life progress. Dramatically greater life progress. Not just restoration, but *evolution that you'll discover is far beyond words!*

The confusion arises when we think of symptom alleviation as the *determinant* of a successful healing: This is a constricted mindset that doesn't allow us, either as practitioner or recipient, to easily remain attachment-free. In it we lose all connection with receiving, all understanding that we are designed to be receivers, designed to be whole and, instead, we are thrust into the constraints of being result-oriented. The reality is, focusing on the healing of symptoms is focusing on the tip of the iceberg, and that limited perspective is precisely what holds us back. It precludes us from *having* entrée *to* the fullness of the greater picture, *our* greater picture. And in this chase, we often overlook the cardinal understanding that focusing on the symptoms can be the strongest *reinforcement* of those symptoms. A Catch-22 situation bypassed in the Reconnective Healing Experience.

Opening the Door

The Reconnective Healer's role is to open the door; the recipient's role is to have the courage to step *through* that door. For the healer, to patiently hold the door open and not devise ways to drag, pull or push the recipient *through* it signals an understanding and integrity that offers the recipient the opportunity and accountability to become his/her own instrument of healing and move forward *in* and *as* pure awareness. Innately, the authentic healer knows they are not there to determine what the recipient receives. That is simply not the healer's role.

What, though, if the recipient chooses to *not* walk through that open door? Might you assume the healing hasn't worked? First of all, how would you know whether the recipient chose to walk through the door *or* whether the healing worked? The only way for you to make *either* assumption is to base it on the outcome you are focused on. And that's hardly an accurate gauge. *Whatever* the recipient comes back with, *whatever* that appears as to you, or even to the recipient at that juncture, *is the healing that's appropriate for them.* It's never really a choice of walking through a door or not, because the choice of whether or not to walk through *that* door *is* a walking through of a door. It may be a different door. Yet it's always a walking through of a door. And it's always a choice.

From what we've witnessed over the years, we've come to realize that Reconnective Healing *always* works. Sometimes it comes in the form you desire, sometimes in a form you haven't even dreamed of, other times at a level that may have been unimaginable to you. Sometimes it seems to show up all at once, sometimes over time, and on rare occasions you may notice little or nothing. And then often it appears when you least expect it. However it shows up, it always works. Quoting the entity Solomon, "By removing your conscious judgment of what you're seeing, and allowing the infinity of that process to enter into your soul, you start to heal—you start to reconnect to that greater connection, to that infinity of what we are. And you begin to access the answers that you need in this plane."

Whatever your focus or initial observable outcome, Reconnective Healing tends to permeate all areas of your life and, as a life force unto itself, accelerates unparalleled positive life progress.

Yes, You *Can* Get Here from There!

...

Hi, Eric here ... Undoubtedly the Reconnective Healing frequencies played and continue to play a major role in my evolution both as a healer and a person.

For Dr. Eric Pearl, the chiropractor, my orientation was to "remove the interference, get out of the way and allow the power that made the body to heal the body." Yet I periodically allowed that pristine consciousness to muddy itself up when I became preoccupied with alleviating my patients' suffering and getting rid of their symptoms. It took a continuous recentering on my part to keep in mind that my highest calling was to *allow* the recipient to heal, not to attempt to force a healing.

When I first assumed the role of a Reconnective Healing practitioner, the clarity with which it presented itself strongly embedded me in the healing consciousness and embedded the consciousness of healing within me. Clients would come in and the very first things they'd tell me about, quite understandably, were their symptoms. Once they got their first symptom out of their mouth, a litany of their other symptoms was waiting in the wings, each to be described and discussed in great detail. Some went as far back as their early childhood, some to their birth and some would attribute them to past lives. Let's face it, we've been raised in a symptom-oriented society. And it's not easy to change that consciousness. Certainly, for most, not in the snap of a finger.

And so my first interaction with clients naturally became one of education. A healer, like any other healthcare provider, is a *teacher*. And I quickly realized that the sooner I understood this, the better off we would all be. I proceeded to explain to my clients that their symptoms were not their actual problems, but merely indicators of an overall imbalance—an imbalance obstructing their ability to live a full and rewarding life. The imbalance was a fire within their corporeal house, and their symptoms, the alarm it was sounding that was demanding their immediate attention. And whether or not we or they knew exactly where the fire was, the intelligence of *IT*—Energy, Light & Information—*did* in fact know. That's what the frequencies were actually addressing: the fire, not the alarm. Once that fire was extinguished, the alarm signaling the imbalance no longer served a purpose, so its propensity was to stop. It's just that simple. *Healing* is just that simple. But it doesn't always serve everyone's financial interest for you to know that.

Did all of my clients grasp this understanding? *No. (And they were in good company, because many healing facilitators also don't seem to grasp this, don't seem to want to grasp this, or, for various reasons, may not really want you to grasp this.)* Did many of them remain fixated on their symptoms? *Yes.* Did many more clients than not gratefully receive this understanding and welcome this progressive, more comprehensive approach? *Absolutely!* Our responsibility as healers is to share information, to educate and to enlighten.

Yet we cannot be responsible for how much of that knowledge and information is accepted and assimilated. Again, we are here to open a door. It is the other person's responsibility to choose to step through that door, *or not.* Just because someone chooses *not* to step through doesn't diminish a healer's responsibility to hold the door open for them. Nor does it diminish their pleasure in holding it wide open for the next person. And always hold it wide and fully open. There is no such thing as holding it *too* wide open. It is only the fear-based ego that feels entitled to attempt to rein it in, to determine how much is right for another person. The role of the facilitator is to open the door and witness. Nothing more, nothing less. Really.

Today's healer has evolved and is continuing to evolve. When a Reconnective Healing session is conducted, a quiet space of stillness arises, shared by and within the client and the healer, resulting in an effortless, unified experience. Through active awareness, the Reconnective Healing facilitator accesses and receives *IT*, shares *IT* with the recipient and, in doing so, ignites healing. Within this newly discovered freedom unfolds more freedom and discovery—discovery of *you*, clearing the path to become consciously aware of That Which Is, being fulfilled.

Think of when you were first learning to drive a car. You had to focus on keeping your hands on the wheel at a ten o'clock and two o'clock or nine o'clock and three o'clock position, maintaining *x* amount of car lengths in accordance with your speed, making sure you could see two headlights in your sideview mirrors before changing lanes, and so on. Yet at some point not too soon after, you were simply driving in "automatic," what some might consider as almost unconsciously, yet in reality you were *highly conscious and aware and everything flowed, highly centered and completely at ease.* You were no longer afraid to change radio stations while you were driving; at times you could even sneak in a glance at your surroundings instead of remaining myopically focused on the placement of your hands and your position on the road. You could even take in the contents of a billboard without the fear of suddenly discovering you were the only eastbound car in a westbound lane. Just the same, *never text while you're driving.* (Your mother told us to say that. She also wants you to put on a sweater. She's feeling a little chilly.) Anyway, you learned to experiment, play and make new discoveries about what works best for you. Essentially, you learned to drive the car while being in a state of *Mindful Mindlessness*. And this was part of your evolution as a driver.

...

You are the Setting. *You* are the Atmosphere.

Now it's time to evolve as a healer. You don't need to find the perfect setting to facilitate a healing because *every* setting *is* perfect: *You* and *everyone* and *everywhere* are perfect. Always. The recipient doesn't *need* to be lying down on a healing or massage table, although that may be optimal and definitely recommended as a first option for professional Reconnective Healing sessions, not to mention highly preferable over being sprawled out across the hood of a '69 VW Bug. Soft lighting and a quiet space are always nice, yet there are no external requirements, no prerequisite settings that have the ability to validate or invalidate, make or break, a healing.

As we are sure you are well aware, however, life happens *in the moment*, and sometimes you are obliged to facilitate a healing *in that moment*, possibly in a public setting, where the space, the sounds, the lighting or the number of people around are not something you can control.

In this situation, as best as you can, direct yourself away from the sights and sounds of that particularly distracting setting and bring your awareness to what you are receiving, feeling and observing. Maintain your attention solely on the person you are working with. This allows you, as the instrument for the Intelligence, to learn to hear your own music. And together you become one: You, the person you're facilitating a Reconnective Healing Experience for, and God, Love, the Intelligence of the Universe. One. And suddenly all distractions disappear, all otherness dissolves, both for you and the person with whom you are interacting. It simply becomes a part of the background tapestry. And a beautiful background tapestry at that, all existing in an ethereal silence that is not a silence.

Let's give you an example.

One day I, Jillian, was sitting in a hair salon waiting to have my hair cut when I heard a young child screaming. She wasn't in the salon itself, her screams were coming from somewhere outside, in the parking lot. Abruptly the front door flew open and in rushed a visibly upset trio of a mother, a grandmother and a young girl, maybe all of four years old. The girl was uncontrollably screaming and crying in pain. Mother and grandmother were frantically trying to distract the child from her torment. Somehow the family car door had accidentally slammed shut on her finger! This was clearly a time to be *present* —not a time to take out an appointment calendar, borrow a pencil and look to see if I could find an available opening for a healing session sometime, possibly, oh, um, let's see ... *Is next Thursday good for you?*

Over the din of the blow-dryers, the strong smell of hair color, the babel of customers and stylists chatting and the music du jour blaring, a busy hair salon might not seem the ideal venue for a healing. Yet, at the same time, *it was just perfect.* I fixed my eyes on the girl and smiled. Everyone else in the salon seemed to disappear, as did the sound. Contact. She looked back. I gently beckoned with my finger, compassionately and knowingly mouthed *Come here.* Through her tears and hysteria, I observed only the briefest moment of contemplation flash across her face. All doubt as to whether she was coming vanished. As her mother and grandmother looked on in wonder, she made her way across the room to me. She was certainty in chaos.

I asked her to hold her hand out while I brought my hands up to either side of hers. I began to feel, find and play with the frequencies. Her fingers immediately started to move on their own. In that moment she stopped crying and alternated between staring at her fingers and staring at me. She was spellbound by what she observed. I smiled again and said, "See that?" as I pointed to her moving fingers.

Awestruck, the little girl whispered a thoughtful, "Yes."

In that interchange, we both shared a moment of mutual fascination and discovery. I say *both* because each person receives the frequencies in a unique and appropriate manner for them. This is part of what makes each RH Experience new—a new healing, a new experience, a new moment.

In that instant, time stood still. Mother and grandmother went silent, as did the rest of the salon. The girl smiled quietly, still as a mouse. She took it all in stride. And, returning to her mother, she went on with her life as if nothing out of the usual had occurred. Me? I waited for my haircut . . . and was in great appreciation of that shared moment.

When we find ourselves distracted while facilitating a RHE, it's a clear indicator that we've allowed our personality or ego to take over, our attention to shift off the person and on to us, that we've made it all about us and positioned ourselves as the dominant or primary character of importance in the healing equation. Often we blame the setting instead of accepting our accountability in the moment. The perfect setting and moment for a healing is always *here*, always *now* . . . and always *you*!

Sometimes we may find ourselves internally asking *when did that healing begin? What was the mechanism that facilitated it?* And if we're feeling truly introspective in that moment, we might even ask ourselves, *Whose healing was it, really?*

It's plausible to say the healing began the moment my situational awareness was triggered. I can assure you, however, that it happened way before I lifted my hands to play with the frequencies and share a Reconnective Healing Experience with my new young acquaintance in the salon. You see, an important part of the healing process was mediated *through our eyes.* Your eyes automatically know how to access the Energy, Light & Information. My eyes and the girl's eyes met . . . and the frequencies automatically knew and found their way home. And our eyes maintained a reciprocal dance of communication throughout our interaction. Yet if you are working with someone who's lying facedown and has their eyes closed, *the reciprocal dance still occurs*!

Ostensibly it was the girl's healing. She saw and experienced something new that will be with her throughout her lifetime. Once you interact with the Energy, Light & Information of the RHE, you are forever changed. It was also a healing for her mother and grandmother, who both observed and experienced healing as a new reality in *their* lives and the lives of their family. For that matter, it was a healing for each person in the salon who chose to witness it.

Lastly, however, it was *my* healing, for I allowed in a new life experience that expanded my understanding and capacity as a healer, and expanded my heart and my essence as a being of love. We carry each one of our healings into our life, into everything we are and do, including into each healing session we facilitate. We carry every healing into our next session. Every healing session allows you to emerge a fuller, deeper version of who you are. Each healing is *our* healing.

Healing and Love are One and the Same

The healer is a combination of many things.
Suffice it to say, none of these things are easily perceptible above the whole.
Like the beating of our hearts,
it occurs without needing to be in our cognizant awareness.
And requires no conscious thought or intention.

The healer is a combination of many things. Suffice it to say, none of these things are easily perceptible above the whole. Understanding this allows you to become more and more the observer and the observed, the seer and the seen, the witness and the witnessed, so you are observation *itself*! You are sight, *itself*! You are witnessing *itself*! Our ultimate existence is awareness. And we are here to learn to exist as awareness more and more. However, a lot of the time we find ourselves in subject/object. When we notice this, let's do so with only a minimal amount of judgment. It would be inauthentic to say without *any* judgment, for there is a certain amount in simply learning to see and observe. This subject/object split keeps us just below our penultimate state, that of awareness itself. Allow yourself to dance into and out of that subject/object split of observer and observed, seer and seen, witness and witnessed into the purity of observation, sight and witnessing.

Healing is nonjudgmental. We don't judge healings as good, bad, better or worse according to whether or not the desired outcome has been attained. There are myriad potential outcomes and manifestations of every healing, and each carries with it its own perfection. Healing comes from you allowing yourself to step into a state of loving detachment. Again, here you are neither the lover nor the loved: here you exist simply, naturally, as *love* itself. In this you release your attachment to the person receiving the healing as well as to the healing outcome. And once we gain this understanding, we find ourselves on a path from which there is little satisfaction in turning back. What matters is that we learn to love others, to give, share, communicate and interact with others in a way that allows them to experience this love. Ultimately, this is us learning to love ourselves. To see ourselves in others, to receive ourselves in others, to love ourselves in others. And to recognize that essentially there *are* no others. True love is *being,* in which we exist as one and everyone, although we may not always be cognizant of it. And we express ourselves in many ways in this being as we continue to grow and evolve in the "Is-ness" of Energy, Light & Information.

Reconnective Healing and love are one and the same. There is no technique in either. In a Reconnective Healing Experience, a minute becomes an hour, an hour a minute. And you are lost in the timeless wonder, the dance of it all. Yet at the same time, you have never been less lost in your life.

All of us are evolving our capacity to receive because we are designed to be receivers. Humanity is designed to receive. And now we can all allow these Reconnective Healing frequencies to place us in a sphere of clarity, presence and freedom, a sphere of healing and love. It is here that we become not only an inspiration for ourselves and for others, but for Energy, Light & Information as well, immersed in and learning the "language" of the Reconnective Healing Experience as our cognitive thinking mind moves aside and reveals what it's been hiding: Each and every one of us is the ultimate instrument for *That Which Is.* As we touched on earlier, we are here to learn how to tune, create, compose and play ourselves so that we may truly heal. *Healing* is learning to *listen,* to experience the new flow of receivership bestowed through this Energy, Light & Information, and to live in your true worthiness, free of the fear-filled cultural and societal impositions that we unwittingly accept.

There is a healer in every one of us. It's not just a profession or a practice. When we allow ourself to see this in everyone, when we recognize even our clients as healers, our nature and relationship with *everyone* changes and comes into full blossom. Everyone is a healer. Everyone benefits from every healing. Everyone. Everywhere. Every time.

Self-Recognition Is the *Only* Recognition That Matters

"You are already there. Your perception is just joining you."

—*Jillian Fleer*

Ask yourself: *Do I really want to continue into a new world of healing by following old protocols and procedures, those of the world before me with its symptom-based and diagnostic focus, a basis used to determine a course of treatment centered on drugs and surgery? Are the protocols, codes, covenants and conventions used by treatment-based approaches really the optimal protocols I want to use for healing today? Or, more likely, have I been on automatic, unconsciously following that approach because I was brought up in an allopathically centered society where I heard commercials telling me that if I have a stuffy nose, I should take this medicine or if I have back pain, I should take that one as they played continuously 24 hours each day in department store elevators and dentist offices, buses and airports, even showing up on smartphones and computers and punctuating news shows and websites. And yet somehow I simply didn't think to question how to move beyond the status quo,* even while progressing into the healing world?

We didn't recognize the automatic programming. Even though we've changed the name of what we're doing, referring to ourselves as healers and thinking that that would be enough to change our consciousness and that of the world around us about healing and healthcare, have we unwittingly found ourselves trapped in a "rinse-repeat" pattern? What if we were able to leave symptom/treatment/therapy-based approaches to those licensed healthcare professionals whose fields are based upon that and we embrace a healing approach better suited for *healing*?

Uniformly, general practitioners as well as specialists and other professionals in mainstream and even alternative/complementary/integrative healthcare have been trained in their particular fields of the healing arts and certified with hard-earned degrees and/or titles: We do not minimize how tough it is to endure the rigors of these educational processes nor how important, vital and rewarding these careers can be. And we're sure these practitioners are appreciative of entering into a field where the work of the earlier pioneers have already blazed a trail for them.

To be a healer, however, can be quite a different thing: You have to find your *own* recognition, you have to *become* your own recognition. A *self-referential* recognition. A recognition that comes from within. The internal that is eternal. And you will find that it's the *only* recognition that *truly* matters. There is little that is more fulfilling in life.

There may, from time to time, arise people or organizations attempting to form entities that want to position themselves as having the authority to license or regulate you as a healer, deigning to grant or deny you recognition should you or should you not follow their rules and/or methodologies. They may even attain legal authority to do so. And if they attain that legal authority, it may become wise or necessary to work within their prescribed framework. This will be a judgment call on your part. These organizations have a tendency to come and go. Their authority exists on the external. It is surface, transient, temporary, existing solely in their own eyes, the eyes of those who may not be able to see beyond that, and in the eyes of the powers that placed them in that position. Ultimately, boards and organizations cannot qualify, disqualify, validate, invalidate or even verify you as a healer at the highest level. The most they may do is recognize that you are already a healer or fail to recognize that. Ultimately, the only recognition of real significance comes from within *you*. Deep within you. Your fabric of knowingness. There are authorities and there are authorities. And then there is a Higher Authority. Know the difference.

To truly embody the concept of *I Am ... the Healer*, especially as a professional, you must embrace yourself as you are, reveal yourself to *yourself* as well as to others, not stand behind a facade, cloaked in someone else's idea of appropriate presentation, practice procedures, ethics and morals. As Solomon says, *you need to unveil your soul.* And no one can do that for you. No one can dictate or tell you how to do that. It is a discovery that can only be made *for* you, *by* you. It shows up not in the voice of want or entitlement, nor in the injustice of hegemony or subjugation, but in the *IS-ness* of the *I AM*.

Here's a quick review of some of the points we discussed in this chapter. Read them carefully and allow them to assimilate.

We learned to move beyond the I and into the I Am. We discovered that being the healer is its own unique reward. We found that the role of the healer requires elevated consciousness and expanded awareness and we explored non-judgmental compassion, presence and immersion in timelessness. We even looked deeply into the question of the responsibility of a healer. We gained the recognition that we are the ultimate healing instrument through the gift of receiving the Reconnective Healing Experience. And that we are observation, we are witnessing, we are freedom, awareness and love. We learned to see ourself as an inspirational catalytic agent in a dynamic triumvirate. And that one of the highest gifts we can give ourself is the willingness to witness the purity of innocence.

We discussed the elegant simplicity of the technique-free healer and that it includes the reveal of your inner being, the harmony *of* your presence *in* your presence. That the only thing that keeps us separate from the elegant embodiment of the healer is fear. We highlighted vulnerability, a natural condition of love, as what allows the unveiling of our soul to another person's soul. We explored how removing the symptoms isn't the same as restoring health, that restoring balance and health, however, likely includes the alleviation of symptoms. That the healer's role is to open the door while the recipient's role is to have the courage to step *through* that door. We found great satisfaction in learning that Reconnective Healing *always* works, sometimes coming in the form you thought you desired, sometimes in a form you hadn't dreamed of and other times occurring at levels previously unimaginable to you.

We found great ease of access in realizing that you are the setting, you are the atmosphere; there are no external requirements, no prerequisite settings or external resources that have the ability to validate or invalidate, make or break a healing, or, for that matter, validate, invalidate, make or break you as a healing facilitator. We learned that we can't assess healings by the outcome that we or others permit themselves to recognize. And that we are designed to be receivers. We realized that self-recognition is the only recognition that matters, and that being a healer is very human indeed.

Exercise 7:
Bringing the Frequencies into Your Daily Life

Now that the Reconnective Healing frequencies of Energy, Light & Information, more familiarly known to you now as *IT*, are vigorously coursing through you, it's time for us to address bringing them into your everyday life. Awareness, of course, is both inherent and imperative—awareness when you stand, awareness when you sit, awareness as you move, awareness when you're simply walking. But also awareness as you *are*. Awareness isn't limited to our cognizant awareness. Awareness isn't limited at all. And if awareness *isn't* limited to something we have to be cognizant of, therefore overlooking the fact that awareness is what we are, cognizant or otherwise, how do we bring it into our everyday life? Think about it. Can we bring something into our everyday life *if it's already there?* This question itself opens a whole can of theoretical worms such as how can we bring something into our everyday life if we're not cognizantly aware of it in the first place? Maybe it's not about bringing something into our everyday life as much as it is about bringing our cognizant attention *to* that something.

And that's assuming that that *something* is a thing at all. What if the thing we are bringing our cognizance to is awareness *itself?* Is being *itself?* And therefore is *"no thing."* At all.

Sometimes when walking, we bring our full awareness to the frequencies in our hands and, in doing so, ever-so-slightly allow the frequencies to move them. Other times we like to bring cognizant awareness to the head. It's our own little inner-secret awareness game. (Of course, now that it's in this book, it's no longer a secret.) In this cognizant awareness, we find we walk and move differently, our center of gravity is readjusted. We sit and stand differently with an enhanced ease, balance and fluidity. Sometimes when sitting, maybe in a car or in our own workspace, we notice our cognitive awareness comes to the frequencies and we observe as they play, vibrate and move around. We feel these frequencies in our inner ears and around our eyes. Sometimes we close our eyes and observe as a gentle, involuntary movement sweeps in. And, after a minute or so, opening our eyes we notice the brightness and clarity of color and vision! An incredible experience.

But eventually our attention floats somewhere else. So has the Energy, Light & Information disappeared? Turned off? Gone somewhere? Somewhere *else?* Is there even a "where" for it to go? Or is the *IS* that is Energy, Light & Information—existence itself, the ever-present *Before-Beyond*—always present because it *is* presence? And therefore is it only our cognizant attention that we allow to come in and out of focus? Only the allowing of our cognizant attention to come in and out of focus? Maybe it's time to let go of the question of "how" and instead observe the "what" so we can recognize the "is." *Our IS.*

This exercise is about our being, our presence, our awareness, and therefore *requires no intentional focus.* No intention *whatsoever.* And in having no intention, we have no fear. No fear of doing it right or wrong. Getting the desired results or not getting them. No fear of loss. No fear of lack. No fear of limitation. No fear of nonexistence. No fear of these or other illusions. No fear. None. The personality, the ego, the I, even cognizance, vanishes. Yet, the *I Am*—That Which Is—IS. It was there before. It is there during. It is there after. Cognizance, like everything, comes and goes. Recognition of it comes and goes. Conscious perception of it comes and goes.

So, with the above in mind, take a walk, a drive, an exploration into your life, your everyday life, and discover your ever-present knowingness of, in and as IS. That Which Is. It's *your* excursion for as long as you want. Enjoy it. Experience it. Become the experience of IT! If someone talks to you, feel free to answer or engage them in conversation or not. It's your choice. If your phone rings, feel free to answer it *if you like*. If your attention wanders on your walk and drifts off onto the beauty of the scenery or a fragrance in the air, allow it to wander. If suddenly you recall that your attention was on the vibrations or sensation you were noticing and suddenly they're not in your cognitive awareness of that, wonderful. Allow yourself to float *in* and *as* the awareness that you are and observe how your cognitive awareness of these sensations comes, goes and returns again. It's only your cognizance of them.

The Energy, Light & Information, like you, *IS*. You are That Which Is. It is only an illusion that Energy, Light & Information, God, Love and the Intelligence of the Universe, Being—by whatever name you choose to call it—and you are *finite*. This exercise reveals the illusion and vanishes it.

1. What did I learn from this chapter?
2. What did I discover from this exercise?
3. What ideas are new to me?
4. What ideas are different than I might have thought?
5. What ideas am I now considering, contemplating?
6. Which ideas feel the most natural to me?
7. Which ideas or concepts do I have the most difficulty with or find the greatest challenge in accepting?

8. Which ideas or concepts do I have the most difficulty with or find the greatest challenge in understanding?

9. Which of my previous beliefs and ideas do I find the greatest challenge in releasing and letting go of?

10. Which ideas and concepts do I find the most freeing and empowering?

11. What has my willingness to not know already allowed me to discover? To become?

12. What might my present willingness to not know allow me to discover in the future? To become?

Please respond to the above with your thoughts, possible answers, explanations, ideas, etc., to the best of your ability.

If you don't know how to answer some of the questions above or just don't have the words, we've designed a fill-in-the-blanks model below to help you.

1. I'm not sure I know, but if I did know, the answer might be _____

2. I don't quite have the words to explain this, but if I did have the words, they might be _____

3. I don't quite have the words to describe this, but if I did have the words, they might be_____

There are many things we accept as givens because our eyes see them as such. And this is the basis for most of science today. And it's very logical. We see distance, and therefore accept it as a given. We see clocks and calendars and accept time as a given. Time, space, distance. We see now and then, you and me, here and there. And for our linear perspectives to make sense of things, we build our theories around them unquestioningly. A nonscientific basis for what we accept as science. How do we support the illusion of separation while our words espouse unity, everything and everyone being one?

The Field, of course. Zero Point Field. This allows our perceptions of time and space to remain intact without requiring us to recognize them as illusions of perspective if they show themselves to be that. Sending. Transmitting. Across a medium or field. All seem to make perfect sense. Like waves in water. Like clouds traveling across the sky. All obvious and accepted from the moment we were born and opened our eyes. How could anyone think to question what we see and feel, what we've built our societies around. Commerce? Farming? What time shall I be over for dinner?

But what if Reconnecting isn't about connecting "again?" What if it couldn't be about connecting again? What if connecting again isn't possible because we've always been connected? Because we've always and only been one? What if it isn't about moving forward? Moving beyond? What if it's about *returning*? Returning to before beyond? What if *that* is our healing? What if the healing is about the recognition of what IS? What has *always* been and *always* IS? Not of what was, but of what *IS*? The Infinite? What if discovering that light within us, that knowingness, the return to the Before-Beyond, is not only an opportunity for us, yet a purpose, a mission, a responsibility we are being offered with accountable integrity, the opportunity to bring the gift of recognizing who we are to EVERY SENTIENT HUMAN BEING ON THIS PLANET? What if the next level of human evolution is dependent on *you*? What if the Universe is looking at *you*?

The answers can be found in the recognition that you are integral to a process that is here in the infinite scope of everpresence.

Closing Suggestions

1. Please revisit the *BEFORE YOU READ ANY FURTHER* section before chapter 1
2. Reread your responses where you were asked to write down *everything you feel, believe or know about healing.* Reread your answers. Do they represent who you are today? Please modify them according to your present understanding. Remember, do not erase anything you write or render it otherwise unreadable.

2. Reread the answers you originally wrote to the questions at the close of each chapter. Do they represent who you are today? Please modify

them according to your present understanding. Remember, do not erase anything you write or render it otherwise unreadable.

3. Repeat steps one and two above in three months, six months, nine months, 12 months, and again each subsequent year for the next five years *or longer if you want to observe a more comprehensive picture of your ongoing growth.* Update your answers as you go along because they, like you, will likely evolve over time. And be sure to *date each of your updates* so you may review your progress when you read through your notes at later times. Some of you may find that a really good annual time to do this is New Year's Day, your birthday or some other significant date in your life. *Remember, do not erase, delete or otherwise obscure or make unreadable your original notes. You will find pleasure and value as you return to read through them in the future.* You will likely find it not only valuable but both interesting and highly enlightening to witness and track your own evolution in your process.

4. Open your calendar and mark the dates you plan to revisit your responses so as to support and chart your continued transformation and unfolding. Put a note on each of these dates for you to review your thoughts. Naturally, you may choose to review them at earlier intervals or whenever you feel like it!

In addition to marking these dates in your calendar, we suggest you also record the dates below here in this book as a reminder for you when you pick up the book again. We encourage you, with each rereading of this book and with each review of your notes, to *look back at your life* and write down what has changed for you. What's changed in your primary, family and other relationships, as well as in your career, your financial prosperity and abundance, your life path, etc.? If you haven't yet recognized the correlation between those changes and what you've received and experienced through the reading of this book, there's a really good chance you soon will.

3 months _____

6 months _____

9 months _____

12 months _____

24 months _____

36 months _____

48 months _____

60 months _____

READ THIS BOOK...
AT LEAST THREE TIMES.

You haven't really read *The Direct Path to Healing* until you've read it three times. As you've already discovered, it's written on an infinite number of levels and there's more to unveil in each reading. More insight—*Energy, Light & Information*—awaiting you. So, *read it again.* Then read it *yet again.* *Write* in it. *Highlight* it. *Review* it. There's more. A *lot* more.

SHARE THIS BOOK!

If you already read and shared *The Reconnection: Heal Others, Heal Yourself,* you will find yourself compelled to share *The Direct Path to Healing.* For everyone who is into consciousness, enlightenment and evolution, for everyone who has a family or friends, for everyone who simply *loves,* *The Direct Path to Healing* is one of the greatest and most appreciated gifts to give or receive. A gift of presence, a gift of reception, a gift of the infinite. So whether you choose to share your copy of *The Direct Path to Healing* or give someone else their very own ... *What you are doing is Reconnecting "strands." What you are doing is Reconnecting "strings." What you are doing is bringing "Light & Information" onto the planet.*

Made in the USA
Monee, IL
01 February 2023

25786042R00085